# Louis Armstrong

*MUSICIAN*

# Black Americans of Achievement

*LEGACY EDITION*

Muhammad Ali

Maya Angelou

Louis Armstrong

Josephine Baker

George Washington Carver

Ray Charles

Johnnie Cochran

Bill Cosby

Frederick Douglass

W.E.B. Du Bois

Jamie Foxx

Aretha Franklin

Marcus Garvey

Savion Glover

Alex Haley

Jimi Hendrix

Gregory Hines

Billie Holiday

Langston Hughes

Jesse Jackson

Magic Johnson

Scott Joplin

Coretta Scott King

Martin Luther King Jr.

Spike Lee

Malcolm X

Bob Marley

Thurgood Marshall

Eddie Murphy

Barack Obama

Jesse Owens

Rosa Parks

Colin Powell

Condoleezza Rice

Paul Robeson

Chris Rock

Al Sharpton

Will Smith

Clarence Thomas

Sojourner Truth

Harriet Tubman

Nat Turner

Madam C.J. Walker

Booker T. Washington

Oprah Winfrey

Stevie Wonder

Tiger Woods

# Louis Armstrong

*MUSICIAN*

Kenneth Partridge

**CHELSEA HOUSE**
*An Infobase Learning Company*

**Louis Armstrong**

Chelsea House
An imprint of Infobase Learning
132 West 31st Street
New York, NY 10001

**Library of Congress Cataloging-in-Publication Data**

Partridge, Kenneth, 1980–
Louis Armstrong : musician / by Kenneth Partridge.
  p.  cm. — (Black Americans of achievement, legacy edition)
Includes bibliographical references and index.
ISBN 978-1-60413-833-7 (hardcover)
1. Armstrong, Louis, 1901–1971.  2. Jazz musicians—United States—Biography.  I. Title.  II. Series.
ML419.A75P37 2011
781.65092—dc22  [B]          2010026881

Chelsea House books are available at special discounts when purchased in bulk quantities for businesses, associations, institutions, or sales promotions. Please call our Special Sales Department in New York at (212) 967-8800 or (800) 322-8755.

You can find Chelsea House on the World Wide Web at http://www.chelseahouse.com.

Text design by Keith Trego
Cover design by Keith Trego
Composition by Keith Trego
Cover printed by Bang Printing, Brainerd, MN
Book printed and bound by Bang Printing, Brainerd, MN
Date printed: January 2011
Printed in the United States of America

10 9 8 7 6 5 4 3 2 1

This book is printed on acid-free paper.

All links and Web addresses were checked and verified to be correct at the time of publication. Because of the dynamic nature of the Web, some addresses and links may have changed since publication and may no longer be valid.

# Contents

# 1

# Late Train to Greatness

**Long before he was "Satchmo the Great"** or a virtuoso horn player or a gregarious, gravelly voiced singer and showman; long before he would become one of the most important and beloved entertainers of the twentieth century, who both revolutionized and legitimized jazz music; long before all of this—Louis Armstrong was just a young man waiting for a train.

The date was August 8, 1922, four days after Armstrong's twenty-first birthday. Due to spotty birth records kept in the poor section of New Orleans where he grew up, the burgeoning jazzman believed he was 22. Regardless of his exact age, Armstrong was young and inexperienced. He had made only a handful of trips outside of his hometown of the Big Easy, performing on riverboats that traveled up and down the Mississippi River.

By the time Armstrong arrived at the station, where he was to catch a train bound for Chicago, he had already had a busy day. That morning, he had played his final gig with the Tuxedo Brass Band, the ensemble with which he had built his reputation as one of the city's best cornet players. (He had not yet switched to trumpet, the instrument that would become his trademark.)

The Tuxedo Brass Band had offered Armstrong steady work and a decent wage, and for a long time, he saw no reason to quit. Shy and not particularly ambitious, he was happy to blow his horn for local audiences and earn the kind of comfortable living that, as a boy growing up on the mean streets of "black Storyville"—a dangerous neighborhood mired in violent crime and unspeakable poverty—must have seemed almost unobtainable.

Indeed, Armstrong might have never left New Orleans had it not been for Joe Oliver, the cornet player who served as his mentor and father figure. Oliver was already an established musician when a teenage Armstrong began playing the seedy honky-tonks of black Storyville. Oliver was a stern, serious man, but he encouraged the youngster, showing him tricks and instilling in him the confidence Armstrong had always lacked.

Oliver was one of the early New Orleans jazzmen to try his luck outside of the city. By 1922, he had settled in Chicago, where he formed the popular Creole Jazz Band. That summer, Oliver decided to add a second cornet to his group's lineup, and in July, he sent a telegram to Armstrong, inviting his protégé to head north. Other bandleaders had tried in vain to lure Armstrong away from home, but given the respect and admiration Armstrong felt for Oliver, he decided to face his fears, pack his things, and leave behind the only life he had ever known.

A crowd assembled that August afternoon to see Armstrong off. As he boarded the train, he carried little more than his horn and a suitcase filled with shabby clothing. Although it was summertime, he wore long underwear—clothing suggested by his mother, a Louisiana native who had heard stories about the Windy City's frigid cold. His mother also gave him a trout-loaf sandwich, a snack he would need on the 800-mile (1,287.4 kilometers) journey, since trains were segregated and dining cars were off-limits to blacks.

## A NEW LIFE

Armstrong's decision to spend the morning playing with the Tuxedo Brass Band meant that he had to take a later-than-planned train to Chicago, and when he arrived at his destination, Oliver—now billing himself as King Oliver—was not there to meet him. As Armstrong walked through the station and took his first look at the bustling metropolis that, for the next two years, would be his home, he was awed by his surroundings.

As he had done in St. Louis, a city he visited on one of his riverboat cruises, Armstrong gawked at the skyscrapers. He was nervous and overdressed, and his forehead likely glistened with the type of heavy sweat that, in later years, he would wipe away with crisp white handkerchiefs—props he would carry onstage at theaters and concert halls around the world.

In 1922, however, international superstardom was still years away, and Armstrong lacked the savvy to find his way out of the station. Luckily, Oliver had hired someone to watch out for Armstrong and to drive the musician to Lincoln Gardens, the Chicago nightspot where the Creole Jazz Band was already onstage, performing its nightly set.

At the time, Lincoln Gardens was the largest and most popular nightclub in Chicago's South Side neighborhood. Although most of the patrons were black, the venue also attracted its share of white jazz fans, some of whom—Benny Goodman, among them—would later become famous musicians.

Arriving at the venue that first afternoon, Armstrong hesitated to go inside. As Oliver's band worked up a fierce, swinging groove, he listened from outside and wrestled with old insecurities, worrying that he was not good enough, that he had gotten in over his head.

King Oliver's Creole Jazz Band was one of the most influential early jazz bands. From left to right, the members are drummer Baby Dodds; trombonist Honore Dutrey; lead trumpeter Joe "King" Oliver *(seated)*; banjo player Bill Johnson; clarinetist Johnny Dodds; cornetist Louis Armstrong; and pianist Lil Hardin. Armstrong later wrote of his mentor: "If it had not been for Joe Oliver, jazz would not be what it is today."

Finally, Oliver came through the front door and dragged Armstrong inside, assuring the timid young horn player that the other musicians were eager to meet him. After the show, they dined on rice and beans, a New Orleans specialty that no doubt comforted Armstrong. Louis later moved into a boarding house where, for the first time in his life, he had his own private bathroom.

## JAMMING WITH THE KING

The following night, Armstrong made his debut with the Creole Jazz Band. His nerves subsided as he took the stage beside Oliver, a moment he would remember for the rest of his life. "When we cracked down on the first note that night at the Lincoln Gardens, I knew that things would go well for me," he wrote in his 1954 memoir, *Satchmo: My Life in New Orleans.* "When Papa Joe began to blow that horn of his it felt right like old times. The first number went over so well that we had to take an encore."

Indeed, the band was so hot that Oliver kept his men onstage a half hour longer than usual. At one point, the King ceded the spotlight to his young heir, letting Armstrong stand out front and "play my rendition of the blues," as Armstrong wrote. "I had hit the big time," Armstrong remembered. "I was up north with the greats. I was playing with my idol, the King, Joe Oliver. My boyhood dream had come true at last."

## THE ROAD AHEAD

Staring into the audience that night at Lincoln Gardens, Armstrong could never have imagined the success that lay ahead. He had no idea that, less than a decade later, he would record a series of songs that would forever change the face of jazz music, or that throughout the 1930s and 1940s, he would become an in-demand bandleader and singer of pop standards able to tour the country—and, indeed, the world—as frequently as he pleased.

The 21-year-old Armstrong certainly could not imagine himself as a "goodwill ambassador," the role he would play in his later years as he crisscrossed the globe, shaking hands with dignitaries, flashing his famous smile. Nor could he have known that, four decades after his debut at Lincoln Gardens, in 1964, his rendition of a Broadway tune called "Hello, Dolly!" would knock the mighty Beatles—the kings of rock 'n' roll, a genre that, in 1922, had not even been invented—out of the top spot on the pop charts.

Indeed, as Armstrong blew his cornet on the Lincoln Gardens stage, he stood on the verge of a remarkable career. Trumpeter, singer, comedian, composer, radio host, TV personality, movie star, and writer—he was to become all of these things and more. His talent was as boundless as his love of entertaining, and for more than a half century, he was never far from his next wave of applause.

# 2

# Growing Up
# in the Battlefield

**Louis Armstrong went his entire** life claiming—and most likely believing—he was born on July 4, 1900. In fact, there were no fireworks displays, no celebrations of any kind, to mark the arrival of the future jazz great.

Baptismal records discovered after the musician's death indicate he was actually born on August 4, 1901. If his mother, Mary Ann, heard a "shooting scrape" the night she delivered, as she later recalled, it was not Independence Day revelry, but rather the kind of gun violence common in "the Battlefield," the rough-and-tumble section of New Orleans where the story of Louis Armstrong begins.

Mary Ann Albert—typically referred to as "Mayann" in Armstrong's writings—was just 15 when she gave birth to Louis, her first and only son. She had moved to New Orleans from nearby Boutte, Louisiana, to escape the sugarcane fields and find work as a housekeeper. Soon after arriving in the city, she met and fell in love with a factory worker named William Armstrong, better known as Willie, and the couple settled into a house on Jane Alley. It was there that arguably the most influential musician, jazz or otherwise, of the twentieth century was born.

The confusion regarding Armstrong's birth date is strange only by modern standards. At the time, records were not kept with the same accuracy they are today, and in such neighborhoods as the Battlefield, where most people—Armstrong's parents included—were poor, black, and illiterate, it was especially unlikely to find reliable birth information. Many people simply chose their own birthdays, and July 4 was a common selection, if for no other reason than it was easy to remember.

## A ROOTLESS CHILDHOOD

Willie abandoned the family soon after Louis's birth, and before long Mayann, too, shirked her parental responsibilities. She left the boy in the care of his paternal grandmother, Josephine, and moved to Perdido Street, located in an area of the city then referred to as "black Storyville."

Even in turn-of-the-century New Orleans, a place where blacks, particularly those with lighter complexions, received slightly better treatment than elsewhere in the South, segregation was a fact of life. Black Storyville was the "colored only" section of Storyville, a red-light district established in 1897 and named for councilman Sidney Story. Both Storyvilles, black and white, were wild places: Alcohol flowed, prostitution was legal, and crime was rampant. Some have speculated that Mayann herself worked as a prostitute, and although Armstrong acknowledges this possibility in *Satchmo: My Life in New Orleans*, he never saw definitive proof.

Regardless of how Mayann made her living, Louis was essentially parentless for the first five or six years of his life. Josephine did her best to care for the boy, teaching him morals and protecting him from the kinds of shady characters—

**A street scene of Storyville, the famed jazz, blues, and red-light district of New Orleans, Louisiana, in the early 1900s. Louis Armstrong would come of age in this wild neighborhood.**

pimps, thieves, and gunmen—that populated the Battlefield. She sent him to kindergarten and accompanied him to church, where he sang gospel songs and got his first taste of music.

Roughly two years after Louis' birth, Willie and Mayann briefly reconciled and had a second child, a girl they named Beatrice. Louis, however, did not meet his sister, whom everyone called Mama Lucy, until 1905 or 1906, when Mayann, having fallen ill, sent a friend back to the Battlefield to retrieve her son. Riding on the streetcar from Jane Alley to Perdido Street, Louis accidentally sat in a whites-only seat, his gaff revealing his ignorance of the day's racist Jim Crow laws.

**A portrait of a young Louis Armstrong with his mother, Mayann *(center)*, and sister, Beatrice, in 1918. Despite the fact that his mother was often absent from his life, Armstrong never had anything but love for her.**

After joining his mother and sister in black Storyville, Louis was forced to grow up fast. Mayann recuperated and resumed working as a housekeeper, but she was prone to disappearing for days at a time. It fell to the boy to take odd jobs and help provide for the family. Faced with abject poverty—there was seldom any meat to go with their red beans and rice—Louis seems never to have harbored any resentment toward his mother. He forgave her indiscretions and saved his disdain for his father, a man he never quite forgave for walking away and starting another family.

## THE SEEDS OF GENIUS

Around the time he was seven, Louis went to work for the Karnofskys, a Jewish family whose kindness would have a tremendous impact on his life. The Karnofskys collected and sold junk on a cart they drove through the streets of New Orleans. Louis would often help out on the route, signaling their arrival by blowing into a cheap tin horn. The Karnofskys did not just employ Louis; they also fed and cared for him. The affection the Karnofskys displayed for him sparked his lifelong fondness for Jewish people, food, and culture. They also loaned him the five dollars he used to buy his first proper instrument, a pawnshop cornet.

Louis was able to play tunes on the cornet—a stubbier cousin of the trumpet—almost from the start. He also showed promise as a singer. By the time he was 12, he had formed a vocal quartet. The group sang for pennies on street corners and earned praise from established musicians. Armstrong furthered his musical education by lurking outside of dicey neighborhood nightspots, or "honky-tonks," and listening to such horn players as Buddy Bolden, Bunk Johnson, and Joe Oliver, the man who would later serve as his mentor.

The music Armstrong would have heard around this time was not jazz per se, although the seeds for that new genre—a New Orleans–born sound that would soon take the nation, and indeed the world, by storm—already had been planted.

The bands in the Storyville brothels largely played the blues, one of the chief ingredients in jazz's rich musical gumbo.

Another was ragtime, which musicians such as Scott Joplin had made popular toward the end of the nineteenth century. Jazz, or "jass," as it was initially called, represented a melding of the two, its defining characteristic a syncopated, "swinging," rhythmic quality that stemmed from musicians playing notes slightly ahead of or behind the beat, creating a propulsive sound conducive to dancing. Critics and musicologists have long debated at what point ragtime became jazz, and a number of influential players—pianist and composer Ferdinand "Jelly Roll" Morton, most notably—claimed to have invented the new style.

## New Orleans

Armstrong's hometown of New Orleans, Louisiana, is an American city unlike any other. Established in 1718 by French settlers, the city was built below sea level on a stretch of swampland located near the mouth of the Mississippi River. New Orleans's earliest inhabitants were French-speaking Catholics, many of whom had relocated from the French colony of Canada, and the city had little connection—economic or otherwise—to the English settlements farther up the Atlantic Coast.

Since New Orleans took its cues from France, not England, the city was not governed by the kinds of strict Protestant morals taught by the Anglican Church. Instead, New Orleans was a freethinking, freewheeling place. People sang, danced, ate, and drank excessively and unapologetically, indulging in vices deemed unacceptable elsewhere on the continent.

French slave ships bound for North America often stopped first in the Caribbean, where they unloaded the bulk of their human cargo. As a result, New Orleans initially lacked slave labor and failed to grow as quickly as other cities in the Deep South. Following the American Revolution, many English planters fled Georgia and the Carolinas and settled in New Orleans, bringing with them an influx of slaves that may have included Armstrong's ancestors.

In 1788 and 1794, New Orleans suffered devastating fires, losing hundreds of buildings. In 1803, French emperor Napoleon Bonaparte sold the city to the United States as part of the Louisiana Purchase. The sale brought a flood of Northern businessmen and entrepreneurs, and as the population both swelled and shifted, the city managed to retain its unique culture and

## A FORTUITOUS ARREST

By 1912, young Louis Armstrong had earned something of a bad reputation. He had dropped out of school, preferring singing to studying. On December 31, as the city celebrated New Year's Eve, Louis stole a revolver from one of his mother's boyfriends and loaded it with blanks. That night, as Armstrong walked up Rampart Street, a neighborhood boy fired a cap pistol in his direction. Armstrong returned fire, so to speak, and promptly felt a pair of arms grip him from behind. The arms belonged to a police officer, and Louis spent the first hours of

traditions. In particular, music and dancing remained vital, especially among blacks, many of whom lacked the education and financial means to pursue other types of entertainment.

Although slavery and racism were facts of life, New Orleans offered blacks better lives than they were liable to lead elsewhere. Rather than toiling in the cotton fields, most slaves worked as housekeepers, and even before the Civil War, many French and Spanish slave owners freed their mixed-race children. These freed individuals gave birth to a subset of New Orleanians known as "Creoles of color," people who, by the mid-eighteenth century, had established middle-class communities.

Creoles of color may have fared better than darker-skinned blacks, but even they were not immune to racism. After the Civil War, and indeed, up through and beyond the time of Armstrong's birth, non-whites of all shades were held in check by oppressive Jim Crow laws. In 1894, Louisiana passed a law stating that anyone with a drop of black blood was considered black, and Creoles suddenly found themselves in the same position as the lower-class black laborers they had once looked down on.

Although blacks and Creoles of color were seen as less than human in the eyes of the law, they often frequented the same bars and brothels as whites. In the city's seedier sections, such as black Storyville, where Armstrong grew up, blacks, whites, and Creoles joined one another in the pursuit of pleasure. The intermingling of their musical traditions would ultimately give birth to jazz, a mix of blues, ragtime, and traditional brass fare, or "sweet music."

1913 in a jail cell. The next morning, a juvenile court judge heard the case, and the incident earned Armstrong his first bit of publicity: "Very few arrests of minors were made Tuesday, and the bookings in the Juvenile Court are not more than average," the *Times-Picayune* reported. "The most serious case was that of Louis Armstrong, a twelve-year-old [sic] negro, who discharged a revolver at Rampart and Perdido Streets. Being an old offender he was sent to the Negro Waif's Home."

As it happened, being sent to the Colored Waif's Home for Boys, as the facility was formally known, was the best thing that could have happened to Armstrong. Joseph Jones, a former soldier known to most as Captain Jones, had founded the home in 1906. Jones was of the opinion that young criminals needed to be rehabilitated, not just locked away with other lawbreakers. Through military-style discipline—the boys were given wooden rifles and made to carry out daily drills—and comprehensive schooling, Jones aimed to keep boys like Louis from becoming lifelong criminals.

Armstrong, who up to this point had lived an unstructured, uncertain life, quickly embraced the school's strict daily routine. Before long, he became interested in playing with the 15-piece Colored Waif's Home Brass Band. At first, director Peter Davis was reluctant to let Louis join, perhaps due to his reputation for bad behavior. By the summer of 1913, however, Davis had relented and welcomed Armstrong into the fold.

## IN HIS OWN WORDS...

From an early age, Louis Armstrong was fond of all types of music. Because he seldom drew distinctions among genres, he was as comfortable performing pop songs and show tunes as he was traditional jazz. Asked once whether jazz was a form of folk music, Satchmo responded with one of his most frequently quoted lines: "Man, all music is folk music. You ain't never heard no horse sing a song, have you?"

Louis moved through a series of instruments, including drums and alto horn, before finally getting his hands on a cornet. He learned from Davis basic technique and appreciation for many kinds of music, including classical, and he later remarked, "Me and music got married at the home."

## FINDING A MENTOR

The Colored Waif's Home Brass Band sometimes played parades around New Orleans, and young Louis delighted in putting on his uniform and marching through the streets. But his time at the home was soon to come to an end. In June 1914, he was dismayed to learn his father had arranged for his release. Leaving the home, Armstrong moved in with Willie and his new wife for a while before returning to his mother's home. Around that time, he was hired to play cornet at a local honky-tonk. The six-month engagement allowed him to meet and befriend a number of important New Orleans musicians, among them Joe Oliver.

Although regarded as a gruff man and an exacting bandleader, Oliver must have seen—or heard—in Louis something he liked. He began tutoring the young musician, building on the foundation of skills Davis had given him at the Colored Waif's Home. Although Louis was learning quickly and show-ing promise, he played with incorrect embouchure, the term used to describe the way horn players hold their instruments against their lips and teeth. He rested the valve of his cornet too low on his upper lip, and this improper technique caused him pain throughout his career. It is among the reasons he focused increasingly on singing as the years wore on.

Even as Louis found steady work in the honky-tonks, he needed to supplement his income. He pushed a coal cart by day and used what money he earned to support the four people now depending on him: himself, his mother, Mama Lucy, and a new addition to the family: Clarence, the son of a cousin who had died soon after childbirth.

In 1917, as the United States entered World War I, New Orleans officials bowed to demands made by the U.S. Department of the Navy and closed down Storyville, ostensibly to keep sailors from visiting the district's prostitutes. Storyville's shuttering had an unintended effect on musicians, who could no longer count on the steady work they had enjoyed in area brothels. Nevertheless, Louis continued to find paying gigs, and after Oliver brought his act to Chicago,

## The Birth of Jazz

It has been said that jazz could not have come from anywhere but New Orleans. This may be true, given the abundance of music, the liberal social climate, and the unique mix of cultures present in the Crescent City at the dawn of the twentieth century.

Although most scholars agree that jazz was born around 1900, its roots stretch back hundreds of years. In the early seventeenth century, as African slaves began arriving in North America, they brought with them native forms of music—diverse sounds that shared at least one thing in common: an emphasis on rhythm. Slave captains often encouraged their captives to sing and dance, lest they die from inactivity or despair.

Upon arriving in the New World, slaves clung to what they could of African culture. Over time, they mixed elements of their own music with European hymnals and dance songs, creating a sound generally referred to as "plantation music." This hybrid style actually comprised numerous subgenres, including "work songs" and "field hollers." From these came blues and ragtime, the precursors of early jazz.

Unlike traditional European music, blues and ragtime allowed for rhythms and melodies that contrasted with one another. Singers and instrumentalists positioned their notes ahead of and behind a song's central beat, creating a propulsive push-and-pull sound. Ragtime differed from blues in that it was built on a "ragged," syncopated rhythm. Whereas blues musicians had the freedom to stretch melodies as they saw fit—sometimes racing ahead of the beat, sometimes falling behind—ragtime demanded that melodic accents fall exactly halfway between beats, creating the rigidity that was its defining characteristic.

By 1900, blues and ragtime had become popular in New Orleans, as had "sweet music," the term given to the expertly played polkas and waltzes favored by well-to-do white listeners. Sweet music was typically played by

Louis took over his mentor's place in the band of trombonist Kid Ory.

## FULL-TIME MUSICIAN

When the war ended in November 1918, Armstrong had extra reason to celebrate: New Orleans would regain its nightlife, and musicians would once more have ample opportunities for paying gigs. On November 11, the day of the armistice, he

classically trained Creoles. At the turn of the century, many of these musicians became enamored of the edgier sounds as they played in the honky-tonks of black Storyville. One such musician was Buddy Bolden, the cornetist some music critics and fans credit with "inventing" jazz.

What Bolden was playing probably was not jazz, but rather a loosened-up form of ragtime that incorporated elements of blues. From this combination of blues and ragtime came the "swinging" quality that is the essence of jazz. For a time, the musicians that followed in Bolden's footsteps and performed the earliest proper jazz songs continued referring to their music as "ragtime." It was not until 1912 that the word *jazz* finally appeared in print, and it would take another five years for the all-white Original Dixieland Jazz Band to cut what is widely considered the genre's first record, *Livery Stable Blues*.

In the early decades of the twentieth century, jazz was considered unsophisticated music, perhaps because it was associated with the brothels and black ghettos from which it came. It did not help that "hot music," as it was sometimes called, had a sexually suggestive quality—the result of its propulsive swing. Of course, it was precisely this trait that made the music so attractive to young people in the 1920s, a decade that would become known as the "Jazz Age."

Jazz soon overcame its stigma to become the preeminent form of popular music in the United States, with the classic New Orleans sound giving way to swing, bebop, and a number of subsequent offshoots. Thanks to such pioneers as Louis Armstrong, jazz went global, inspiring musicians and winning fans around the world. Starting in the late 1950s, rock 'n' roll began to surpass jazz as America's most popular form of music, but not before a number of innovative composers and soloists—Armstrong chief among them—had finally made jazz a respected art form.

quit his job with the coal company, abandoning his wagon and mule on the side of the road. Around this time, he married a former prostitute named Daisy Parker, the first of his four wives. She was prone to jealousy and violence, and although the couple would remain married for four years, they spent much of that time apart.

Armstrong's stint as cornet player in Ory's group lasted until 1919, when the bandleader left New Orleans for Los Angeles. Ory had initially made the cross-country journey for health reasons—a doctor recommended a drier climate for his lungs—but before long, he realized money could be made playing jazz music on the West Coast, where audiences had never heard such a sound. He sent for his old band members, but Armstrong declined the invitation.

His reluctance might have had to do with the fact that Joe Lindsey, another member of Ory's group, opted to stay home, lest he incur the wrath of his girlfriend. Armstrong may have been driven by more than just loyalty, however: At the time, he lived a sheltered existence. He had never been away from home and, as talented as he was, he lacked the confidence to simply pack his things and leave behind the only life he had ever known.

## ROLLING ON A RIVER

What happened next was the result of Fate—literally. Fate Marable was a Kentucky-born pianist and bandleader hired by brothers Roy, Joe, John, and Verne Streckfus to perform on their Mississippi River excursion boats. The ships made pleasure cruises up and down the river, some carrying as many as 5,000 passengers. Marable did not start out playing jazz, but he encountered the music on his frequent trips to New Orleans. In 1917, as early recordings made by the Original Dixieland Jazz Band were gaining popularity and introducing jazz to the nation, Marable changed over to the new "hot" music, as it was known.

Joe Streckfus was a demanding boss and self-styled music authority. He would only hire the best of the best—players who could read music and keep impeccable time. Nevertheless, he gave Marable license to staff his own band, and it was likely only for this reason that Armstrong landed a job. Although he could not yet read music, he was a self-taught phenomenon. That Marable—a strict boss in his own right—hired Armstrong after hearing him play with Ory is proof that, even in his late teens, Armstrong was doing something different, playing with a clear, sharp tone and swinging notes in ways no one else could.

Armstrong most likely played "moonlight cruises" with Marable in 1918, while still part of Ory's band, but in the summer of 1919, the young cornet player was offered a job aboard the SS *Sidney*, a riverboat that would cruise from St. Louis to Minneapolis. Armstrong jumped at the chance, although he was less than prepared for the world outside of the New Orleans ghetto. As a shy boy in faded overalls, he was dumbfounded by the St. Louis skyline. "What are all those tall buildings?" he asked Marable. "Colleges?"

That summer would prove monumental for Armstrong. Under Marable's direction, he learned to read music and improvise solos. Marable and Streckfus required their musicians to be dapper dressers, and Louis traded his tattered country-boy clothes for a crisp suit. He also gained weight and caught a bad cold that, according to some, left him with the hoarse voice that would become his trademark. Finally, Armstrong left the cruise; some said he quit, having grown tired of Marable's rules, while others—the bandleader included—insisted he was fired.

### LEAVING HOME

Upon returning to New Orleans, Armstrong became a full-time member of the Tuxedo Brass Band. These were happy days for Armstrong: Thanks to the education he had received aboard Marable's riverboat, he was feeling more confident in his abilities, blowing the high C notes for which he would later become known. The Tuxedo Brass Band had a steady, well-paying gig at Tom Anderson's New Cabaret and Restaurant, and Armstrong was making double what he had with Ory's group. He was also earning a reputation as one of New Orleans's top jazz players. Only one thing—or one man, rather—could make him give up the comfort of this situation and leave New Orleans.

In July 1922, Armstrong received a telegram from Joe Oliver, the man he lovingly referred to as "Papa Joe." Oliver was looking to add a second cornet to the Creole Jazz Band, the group he had started in Chicago, and wanted Armstrong to head north. Others had attempted to lure Armstrong out of the Big Easy—in addition to Ory's California offer, New York City-based bandleader Fletcher Henderson had tried to nab Armstrong for his ensemble—but only Oliver wielded the kind of influence that would set the young man packing. "Joe Oliver is my idol," Armstrong said. "I have loved him all my life. He sent for me and whatever he's doing I want to do it with him."

Weeks later, on August 8, Armstrong played his final gig, a traditional New Orleans "jazz funeral," with the Tuxedo Brass Band. When it was finished, he went home, threw what little clothing he had into a suitcase, and headed for the train station, Mayann's trout sandwich in hand. The friends and admirers there to bid Armstrong farewell would wait nearly a decade for the jazzman to return.

# 3

# Making His Name

**Young Louis Armstrong arrived in** Chicago uncultured and untested. Whatever style he had developed on the SS *Sidney* was apparently gone. Pianist Lil Hardin, another new member of Joe Oliver's group, was struck by his less-than-fashionable attire. "Everything he had on was too small for him," she said, as quoted in James Lincoln Collier's *Louis Armstrong: An American Genius*. "His atrocious tie was dangling down over his protruding stomach and to top it off, he had a hairdo that called for bangs, and I do mean bangs. Bangs that jutted over his forehead like a frayed canopy. All the musicians called him Little Louis, and he weighed 226 pounds."

Luckily, he was a snappier cornet player than he was a dresser—not that the audiences at Lincoln Gardens, the popular Chicago club where the Creole Jazz Band was booked, had much chance to hear what he was truly capable of. Although Armstrong had by this time surpassed Oliver in terms of musicianship, he was unwilling to overshadow his mentor. "I never tried to go over him, because Papa Joe was the man and I felt any glory that should come to me must go to him—I wanted him to have all the praise," Armstrong wrote in *Satchmo: My Life in New Orleans*.

Whether Armstrong was in the spotlight or not, the Chicago gamble had paid off. He was now working with his idol and sharing the bandstand with a group of musicians he liked and admired. The nightly gigs at Lincoln Gardens felt more like play than work, and Oliver and his wife, Stella, kept close watch over "Little Louis," treating him like a son.

## FIRST RECORDINGS

On April 6, 1923, Armstrong and the Creole Jazz Band traveled to Richmond, Indiana, where they cut the first in a series of 37 songs they would record by year's end. The session, commissioned by the Gennett label, has since become the stuff of jazz legend. So powerful was Armstrong's playing, the story goes, that he had to stand 20 feet (6 meters) behind the rest of the band—otherwise, he would have drowned out the other musicians.

This is a dubious story for many reasons, but the fact remains that recording technology in the early 1920s left a lot to be desired. Electronic microphones had not yet entered the picture, and the members of Oliver's band would have had to position themselves around an acoustic horn that picked up the vibrations emanating from their instruments. This approach tended to produce muddy recordings, at least by modern standards, and no matter where Armstrong—or anyone, for that matter—stood, the group was unlikely to get a clear sound.

Despite their somewhat crude sound, the early Creole Jazz Band sides have been described by critics as harbingers of Armstrong's eventual greatness. Jazz was not yet an improviser's art form, and even though Oliver believed that horn players should stick to playing straightforward, recognizable

# Chicago

After New Orleans, Chicago was perhaps the most important city in the development of early jazz. Even before Armstrong arrived in 1922, the Windy City boasted a bustling live music scene, where such luminaries as King Oliver and Jelly Roll Morton played regularly to enthusiastic audiences. Gangsters controlled the city's nightlife, and amid rampant gambling, gunplay, illegal drinking—this was, after all, the era of Prohibition—and other thrills, "hot music" was the perfect soundtrack.

Jazz's popularity was partially a result of Chicago's booming African-American population. In the beginning of the twentieth century, many Southern blacks joined the "Great Migration" northward, flocking to such cities as Chicago, Detroit, and New York in search of jobs and better lives. In 1910, Chicago was home to just 44,000 blacks; by 1930, that figure had ballooned to 233,000.

Although Chicago, which had suffered deadly race riots in 1919, was hardly the "promised land" advertised by the *Chicago Defender*, the nation's leading black daily newspaper, it was more hospitable to blacks than the Deep South. Many new arrivals settled in the "Black Belt" section of the city's South Side neighborhood. By the 1920s, African Americans had "more political power in Chicago than anywhere else in the country," Allan H. Spear wrote in *Black Chicago: The Making of a Negro Ghetto*.

The Black Belt was more rundown than predominately white sections of the South Side, but the blacks who lived there tended to have jobs and spend money. They were among the earliest champions of jazz, although white fans also found their way to the neighborhood's nightspots. Many of these clubs were "black and tans," venues that catered to both black and white patrons.

In *Crazeology: The Autobiography of a Chicago Jazzman*, the saxophonist and bandleader Bud Freeman, a member of the Austin High School Gang (a group of young white musicians that went on to become esteemed jazz players), recalled visiting Lincoln Gardens, where Armstrong made his debut in 1922 with the Creole Jazz Band. "Aspiring white jazz musicians used to go there all the time, and the people there were wonderful," Freeman wrote. "They paid no attention to us; they knew we were there to hear the music."

Although jazz had, by this time, also taken hold in New York City, Big Apple musicians had not yet mastered the new sound. Satchmo arrived in 1924 and immediately made his mark on the city. Fletcher Henderson, as quoted in Terry Teachout's *Pops: A Life of Louis Armstrong*, once said that Armstrong made his band "really swing-conscious with that New Orleans style of his." In *Satchmo: The Genius of Louis Armstrong*, Gary Giddins wrote, "He taught New York to swing."

A portrait of Louis Armstrong as a young jazz musician. Early in his career, he tended to underplay to avoid showing up his bandleader and mentor, King Oliver.

melodies, Armstrong found ways to express his creativity. His two solo choruses on "Chimes Blues," cut during the first Gennett date, are held in high regard by critics, as are the duets he and Oliver repeatedly play during "breaks," or portions of the songs where the other instruments drop out.

Armstrong and Oliver had worked out a unique system for rehearsing their patented duets. During live shows, the bandleader would turn to his protégé midway through a number and silently move his cornet valves, indicating the run of notes he would play during the coming break. Armstrong would then come up with a complementary line. For as well as the two worked together, theirs was no longer an equal partnership. Armstrong was capable of playing faster, higher, and more complex parts, but his loyalty to Oliver prevented him from doing so.

Not that Armstrong particularly minded holding back. At this stage in his career, he had no desire to lead his own band. If underplaying was what it took to continue performing with Oliver, the closest thing to a father he had ever had, he was happy to do so. It was more of a problem for Lil Hardin, with whom, by 1923, he had become romantically involved. In August of that year, Armstrong divorced Daisy. He married Lil on February 5, 1924.

Lillian Hardin was from a middle-class black family in Memphis, and what she lacked in musical ability—the general consensus is that she was a merely passable jazz pianist—she made up for in ambition. She could tolerate her new husband's lack of drive no more than she could put up with his shoddy wardrobe, and her efforts to remake Armstrong included more than just buying him new clothes. She convinced him Oliver was stealing his money and holding him back. She then upped the ante with an ultimatum: Find a new band or find a new wife.

For Armstrong, a genial man who spent his life avoiding confrontation, this was a difficult decision. "I never cared to become a band leader: there was too much quarreling over petty money matters," he wrote in *Satchmo: My Life in New Orleans.* "I just wanted to blow my horn peacefully." As much as it pained him to do so, he finally gave in to Lil's demands and quit the group, but he sent another musician to give Oliver the news.

Armstrong quickly found a job with Ollie Powers, a drummer and bandleader whose single-cornet lineup gave Armstrong his first taste of the limelight. The band was booked at the Dreamland Café, another trendy Chicago jazz spot. Armstrong's profile was at an all-time high. And thanks to a fan he had made several years earlier, it was about to get a whole lot higher.

# 4

# Swinging in New York

**In 1922, Fletcher Henderson** had tried in vain to hire Louis Armstrong. Then, in the summer of 1924, the New York City bandleader approached the young cornetist with a more attractive offer. Henderson's orchestra had just become the house band at the Roseland Ballroom, one of New York City's top clubs, and the leader wanted a horn player who could play the kind of "hot" solos the city's growing throngs of jazz fans were starting to demand.

To Henderson, jazz was not something that came naturally. A light-skinned and middle-class native of Cuthbert, Georgia, he grew up far removed from the honky-tonks that had spawned the genre. He learned piano from his mother, a music teacher, and studied chemistry at Atlanta University. After graduation, he moved to New York City, where he wound up working for the nation's first black-owned record company, Black Swan. Touring New Orleans in 1922, Henderson happened to catch one of Armstrong's sets and was impressed by what he heard. When he began looking for a jazzman to bolster his Roseland crew, he knew where to turn.

"I never forgot that kid," Henderson said, as quoted in *Hear Me Talkin' to Ya: The Story of Jazz as Told by the Men Who Made It* by Nat Shapiro and Nat Hentoff. Henderson recalled:

> Louis was even better than Oliver and let no man tell you differently. . . . Knowing the way that horn sounded, I had to try to get him for my band that was scheduled to open at the Roseland Ballroom. Truthfully, I didn't expect him to accept the offer and I was very surprised when he came to New York and joined us.

## NOT QUITE JAZZ

Armstrong did accept the job, arriving in New York City in September 1924. The Big Apple had no shortage of nightclubs and speakeasies—venues that sold alcohol, despite federal prohibition laws—and musicians were always in demand. A number of groups were playing music they termed "jazz," but by and large, these East Coast outfits had not yet learned to swing like their counterparts in New Orleans and Chicago. Bands like Henderson's specialized in the kind of more conventional dance music—foxtrots and the like—preferred by white audiences. They peppered their arrangements with jazzlike flourishes, but it would take Armstrong to really get Manhattan swinging.

If a lack of swing was their only crime, Henderson's musicians might have made a decent impression on Armstrong. The band members were flashy dressers prone to drinking and fooling around onstage. Like their leader, they never had to scrape and claw their way out of dire poverty. Armstrong, having made it all the way from the Battlefield to Broadway, took his music extremely seriously and expected the same from his colleagues.

**A photo of Fletcher Henderson's orchestra in New York, circa 1924. This incarnation of the band features Henderson *(seated at piano)* and Louis Armstrong on cornet *(center, back)*. From left to right the saxophonists are the great Coleman Hawkins, Buster Bailey, and Don Redman.**

Despite having been on the receiving end of Lil's image makeover, Armstrong arrived in New York looking decidedly less than hip. Henderson's drummer later recalled that the cornetist wore long underwear and clunky black shoes. He also carried with him the self-doubt that had plagued him since his New Orleans days. In fact, during his first rehearsal with Henderson's men, he flubbed several of his parts. Although he could read music, he was out of practice. When he came to a passage marked "pp," short for "pianissimo," an indication that the band should soften its playing, Armstrong blew his horn at full strength. Henderson asked Armstrong if he knew what the abbreviation meant, to which the youngster replied, "Why, it means *pound plenty*!"

After shows, while his bandmates played cards, Armstrong would often jam with members of Sam Lanin's group, the all-white ensemble that shared the bill at Roseland. Armstrong was always interested in learning new tricks and techniques. As he grew more confident, he longed to play increasingly adventurous solos and focus more on singing, something he had loved since boyhood and done only sporadically with Oliver's band. Henderson, who encouraged neither Armstrong's soloing nor singing, preferred his musicians to stay within the rigid boundaries set by Don Redman, the band's arranger.

If Armstrong felt artistically stifled, he did not say so. Ever his easygoing self, he was willing to put up with almost anything, so long as it meant he could make a living playing his horn. His insatiable craving for applause had less to do with ego than a need for validation. Once again, it would take Lil to push her husband into the next phase of his career.

## HIS NAME IN LIGHTS

Lil had always felt Armstrong deserved top billing. While he was in New York, she stayed in Chicago and set out to find him a job that would give him just that. She approached Bill Bottoms, the owner of the Dreamland Café, with a proposition, as well as a list of demands: Armstrong would play his club, but only as a headline performer earning $75 per week. Hardin also insisted her husband be billed as "the world's greatest cornet player." When Bottoms agreed, Lil sent a telegram to Armstrong, calling him back to the Windy City.

In a repeat of the incident that had brought about his departure from Oliver's band, Armstrong was once again forced to choose between his boss and his wife. Given that he felt for Henderson none of the love and admiration he had felt

**A portrait of the legendary American blues singer Bessie Smith, circa 1923. Louis Armstrong recorded a number of songs with Smith early in his career, most notably "St. Louis Blues."**

for Oliver, this was an easy call. He gave Henderson his notice and boarded a train for Chicago in November 1925.

Despite his problems with Henderson's men, Armstrong had plenty to show for his time in New York. Over the course of 14 months, he and the band had recorded some 40 sides, 15 of which featured cornet solos. One standout, "Sugarfoot Stomp," marked the first time Henderson's musicians truly mastered the swinging sound of jazz. "That recording was the record that made Fletcher Henderson nationally known," Redman said, according to Collier.

On "Sugarfoot Stomp"—a reworking of King Oliver's "Dippermouth Blues"—Armstrong demonstrates an artistry that, even then, set him apart from his peers. He contrasts the peppiness of Henderson's band by playing in a mournful style. According to Collier, the tune finds Armstrong "captured by an intensifying blue mood." The uncharacteristic "growl" he employs in the tenth bar of the second chorus "express[es] the deepening poignancy," Collier wrote. "It is superb blues playing."

During his time in New York, Armstrong also served as an accompanist on a series of recordings made by female blues singers, including Bertha Hill, Ma Rainey, and Bessie Smith, the so-called "Empress of the Blues." Although these sides are among the more obscure in Armstrong's discography, some, such as the version of "St. Louis Blues" he recorded with Smith, are regarded as blues classics.

Sitting in with composer and musical entrepreneur Clarence Williams and his Blue Five and Red Onion Jazz Babies bands— two groups that, due to their overlapping lineups, were essentially the same outfit—Armstrong recorded an additional two dozen sides that are now regarded as early jazz classics. Several of the Williams sessions paired Armstrong with New Orleans–born soprano saxophonist Sidney Bechet, one of the few musicians then able to play jazz at his level. Critics have long praised the interplay between Armstrong and Bechet. On such tunes as "Cake Walkin' Babies from Home," the jazzmen go out of their way to one-up each other—grateful, no doubt, to finally have some real competition.

# 5

# Hotter Than That:
# A Genius Emerges

**When Louis Armstrong returned to Chicago,** he joined Madame Lil Armstrong's Dreamland Syncopators, the band his wife had put together for the Dreamland Café residency. Although a reporter for the *Chicago Defender* referred to Armstrong as a "famous cornetist" in a story announcing the group's debut, Armstrong was not yet a celebrity. His fan base, insofar as he had one, comprised mostly fellow musicians—players who, thanks to a surge in the popularity of "hot music," could suddenly find work in nightclubs throughout the city. Most, if not all, of these clubs were run by mobsters, men who used violence to intimidate both rivals and the musicians in their employ.

## THE HOT FIVES

The Dreamland Syncopators made their debut on November 6, 1925. Six days later, Armstrong, Lil, and three other musicians—banjoist Johnny St. Cyr, clarinetist Johnny Dodds, and

Kid Ory (the trombonist who had given Armstrong one of his first jobs back in New Orleans)—made their first batch of recordings for OKeh Records, with whom Armstrong had signed an exclusive contract before leaving New York.

The quintet dubbed itself Louis Armstrong and His Hot Five. Over the next few years, with occasional changes to the lineup and group name, this Armstrong-led band recorded a series of sides that would become known as the Hot Fives and Hot Sevens.

The Hot Fives and Sevens stand as the most critically revered recordings of the early jazz period. No longer stifled by Henderson's stiff arrangements, Armstrong cut loose, experimenting with complex solos and playing to the full extent of his considerable abilities. The group was initially nervous, but during its first OKeh session, it managed to record the memorable "Gut Bucket Blues," a tune written and named on the fly.

On the record, Armstrong can be heard gleefully encouraging his bandmates, crying out, "Whip it, kid!" and "Blow that thing, Mr. Johnny Dodds." The band included neither bass nor drums, as OKeh's Chicago studio was ill-equipped to record such instruments, but even without a proper rhythm section, the Hot Five found their swing, capturing what Armstrong called "the New Orleans groove."

On "Heebie Jeebies," another notable Hot Five side recorded three months later, Armstrong "scat-sings" the second verse, swapping the song's actual lyrics for a string of nonsense words. Armstrong maintained that the scatting was accidental, as he had dropped the lyrics sheet and did not want to ruin what was shaping up to be a good take. Whether the story is true, such singing—made all the more distinctive by his sandpapery voice—became an Armstrong trademark, helping him differentiate himself from the scores of jazz singers with less unique voices.

Armstrong the bandleader, like Armstrong the man, was affable and good-natured. Because he preferred to keep

*Louis Armstrong's Hot Five, Exclusive Okeh Record Artists.*

**A 1925 photo of Louis Armstrong's Hot Fives in Chicago, Illinois. From left to right are Louis Armstrong; banjo player Johnny St. Cyr; saxophonist Johnny Dodds; trombonist Kid Ory; and Armstrong's second wife, the pianist Lil Hardin.**

things loose and carefree, Armstrong, along with the other musicians, seldom bothered to write down his arrangements. They practiced in Armstrong's living room and gamely entered the studio whenever OKeh needed new product. The sessions were as informal as the rehearsals, and the band would generally record after running through a new tune no more than a couple of times. Hardin and Armstrong wrote some of the material, at times penning five or six tunes in a single evening.

# Minstrel Shows

Louis Armstrong grew up at the tail end of the "minstrel show" era, a fact one must consider when assessing certain aspects of his career. Often referred to as the first uniquely American form of theater, minstrel shows emerged in the early nineteenth century, as white performers began painting their faces black and outlining their lips in white or red and staging variety shows whose characters were based on crude black stereotypes.

Wearing "blackface" makeup, often created using grease paint or burned cork, minstrel performers tended to portray blacks as lazy, ignorant, and clownish. The shows featured singing, dancing, and comedy skits, and until the early twentieth century, they enjoyed massive popularity, becoming for a time the nation's preeminent form of entertainment.

Although historically it has been easy to dismiss minstrelsy as mean-spirited and racist—and it often was—scholars now view the phenomenon as something more complex. True, white performers made fun of blacks, but the enthusiasm with which they sang and danced was indicative, some argue, of a genuine desire to act like African-American subjects. Imitation, in other words, may have been a form of flattery.

It should also be noted that whites were not the only minstrel-show performers. Black performers also got in on the act, and even though they lampooned their own culture, their performances contained elements of self-empowerment. For the first time, they were able to gain acceptance as entertainers.

Armstrong, by virtue of being born when he was, was familiar with many of minstrelsy's hallmarks. As early as the 1920s, when he began cutting his seminal Hot Five sides, he incorporated some of these elements into his music. He would record novelty songs and tell silly jokes, and onstage, he would mug and roll his eyes, leading some to accuse him of "tomming," or acting like a buffoon.

Later, when Armstrong made the transition to feature films, he was not above singing a song like "Skeleton in the Closet," his big number from his 1936 Hollywood debut, *Pennies from Heaven*. The tune required Armstrong to poke fun at the notion of African Americans being afraid of ghosts, and he dutifully played along, oblivious to how future generations might view his performance.

The key, Armstrong's supporters argue, is to resist judging his work based on modern-day social conditions. By today's standards, some of his songs and film roles are racially condescending. In his time, however, they were completely acceptable. Even if he had disagreed with minstrelsy and its legacy, there was little he could have done. Black performers were not yet in positions to speak out against their white managers, record producers, and studio bosses.

Although the Hot Fives feature incredibly sophisticated cornet playing and mark the point at which jazz went from being ensemble music to a soloist's art form, Armstrong never strove solely for technical brilliance. Even at this stage in his career, he thought of himself as an entertainer, not just a jazz musician, and he and the band were prone to recording short comedy skits and novelty tunes. Although some African-American musicians would later accuse Armstrong of "tomming," or acting like a buffoon to endear himself to white audiences, his act was very much in line with the general sensibilities of the 1920s. He, like many of the day's performers (both black and white), had come out of the minstrel-show tradition and never thought he was degrading himself or his people. He simply wanted to play music that would make people smile.

The Hot Fives certainly did that. Priced at $0.75 apiece, the records sold well, inspiring a new generation of jazz musicians. Armstrong earned $50 per side, and by 1927, he had become famous enough that the Melrose Music Company decided to publish two books of his music, *125 Jazz Breaks for Cornet* and *50 Hot Choruses for Cornet*. The volumes contained transcriptions of solos Armstrong recorded on cylinders specifically for the publisher.

## DOUBLE DUTY

When not in the studio, Armstrong kept busy with two performance bands: Hardin's Dreamland ensemble and the "Little Symphony," a 15-piece outfit that worked the Vendome Theater, a 13,000-seat movie house in Chicago's South Side. Armstrong had been looking for an opportunity to play classical music, and under the direction of Erskine Tate, a violinist and conductor he admiringly referred to as "Professor," he got his chance.

In addition to performing classical material, Tate's orchestra provided accompaniment for the Vendome's silent movies and played pop songs during intermissions. On the "hot" selections, Armstrong would sometimes blow 50 high-C notes in succession, drawing wild applause from the audience. It was around this time that he switched from cornet to trumpet, the instrument with which he will forever be associated. Although the two instruments are virtually identical, the trumpet has a slightly crisper, sharper tone, which may have been why Tate suggested he make the change.

If Armstrong captivated the Vendome clientele, at least one regular theatergoer had a similar effect on him. In 1926, he began dating Alpha Smith, an attractive teenager who often sat in the front row during Armstrong's performances. The jazzman was no stranger to extramarital affairs—in New York, he had dated a chorus girl named Fanny Cotton.

At the time Armstrong met Smith, his marriage to Lil had begun falling apart. The rift was partially due to money and the very different ways Lil and Armstrong had grown up. Having been raised middle class, Lil was used to having nice things. She was the one who had purchased the 11-room house they called home; she managed the couple's business and made all of their financial decisions. Given that the Dreamland band bore her name, Armstrong, "the world's greatest cornet player" or not, was essentially her employee.

Other musicians began to call Armstrong "Henpeck," implying he was controlled by his wife. The couple argued frequently, and Lil later admitted that she had tried too hard to sand down her husband's rough edges and turn him into the kind of respectable man she thought he should be. "We were always Fussing and threatening to Break up if I sat on the Bed after it was made up," Armstrong wrote in a notebook entry reproduced in *Louis Armstrong, In His Own Words.*

With Alpha, Armstrong enjoyed a reprieve from Lil's constant nagging. A poor girl, Alpha had no intention of molding him into something he was not. In the spring of 1926, Armstrong decided enough was enough. He left his wife, moved in with Alpha, and quit the Dreamland band. Despite these developments, Lil continued her professional relationship with Armstrong, playing on subsequent Hot Five recordings.

## UNCROWNING THE KING

It did not take long for Armstrong to find a new gig with the band Carroll Dickerson was leading at the Sunset Café, one of Chicago's "black and tans," or clubs that catered to both black and white patrons. The Sunset was located across the street from the Plantation Club, where King Oliver happened to be playing a residency with his new outfit, the Dixie Syncopators. The proximity spurred competition between the two jazzmen. One night, Armstrong and Oliver faced off on the Sunset's stage, feverishly trading choruses of "Tiger Rag." The cornetist Wild Bill Davison witnessed the musical duel and estimated they went back and forth 125 times. He called it "the most exciting thing I ever heard in my life," according to Burton W. Peretti in *The Creation of Jazz: Music, Race, and Culture in Urban America.*

However evenly matched they may have seemed that night, Armstrong won the battle of the box office, siphoning crowds away from his former mentor. Armstrong's star power was not lost on the Sunset's manager, Joe Glaser, who soon fired Dickerson and rechristened the band "Louis Armstrong and His Sunset Stompers." Such was Armstrong's introduction to Glaser, a man who would later become his manager and serve in that capacity for the remainder of his life.

At the time, Glaser was a small-time gangster known to associate with Chicago organized-crime kingpin Al Capone. Having grown up in a neighborhood rife with underworld characters, Armstrong had little problem with Glaser's mob ties and especially appreciated Glaser's loyalty—something the club manager demonstrated when Capone demanded he take Armstrong's name down from the Sunset marquee. Capone apparently thought Armstrong was not famous enough to warrant his lofty billing. Glaser stood firm, telling Capone that his bandleader truly was the "World's Greatest Trumpeter," as the sign indicated, and that there was no way he was going to change the wording.

## CONSUMMATE SHOWMAN

As leader of the Sunset Stompers, Armstrong presided over a full-fledged variety show, one that featured comedians, dancing girls, and other acts. The show became a sensation, attracting music fans and fellow performers alike. Among those won over by Armstrong's musical and comedic abilities was Bing Crosby, then the singer for Chicago's acclaimed Paul Whiteman Orchestra. He and Armstrong soon became close friends. When Crosby made the jump to major motion pictures, en route to becoming one of the twentieth century's most successful entertainers, he used his influence in Hollywood to help Armstrong do likewise.

The Stompers were more a performance band than a studio one—in the entire time they were together, they cut only one side—but Armstrong kept busy playing after-hours clubs and recording with the Hot Five. In May 1927, after a six-month break, the group returned to OKeh's studios. Armstrong and company took advantage of the label's new electrical recording setup and added a tuba and bass. Over the course of eight days, the expanded lineup rode a wave of creativity and cut the 11 sides that would become known as the Hot Sevens.

Of the many Hot Sevens now seen as classics, "Potato Head Blues" is perhaps the most revered. Of particular note is Armstrong's solo, which strayed completely from the tune's melody. As the band plays a "stop time" chorus—one in which the musicians strike staccato chords every other measure—Armstrong "flings a tune that links the chords together like a cable strung along a row of telephone poles," biographer Terry Teachout wrote in *Pops: A Life of Louis Armstrong*. His playing is both fluid and inventive, and even if the passage was composed in advance, as Armstrong's greatest solos often

**Singer Bing Crosby and Louis Armstrong were good friends and great admirers of each other's work, going back to Crosby's days with the Paul Whiteman Orchestra in Chicago. During their decades-long friendship, they would make a number of movies and recordings together.**

were, it is still considered one of the finest performances in jazz history.

Amid Armstrong's professional triumphs came a devastating personal setback. That summer, his mother, Mayann, died in New Orleans. Armstrong, who had always been close to his mother, later said her death was the only time he ever cried. On her deathbed, Mayann urged Armstrong to "Carry on, you're a good boy." The musician did just that, and as 1927 drew to a close, he and the Hot Five—a quintet once again, having ditched the tuba and drums—cut a number of now-famous sides, including "Struttin' With Some Barbecue," "Savoy Blues," and "Hotter Than That."

"Hotter Than That" was one of several Hot Fives recorded with a sixth band member, Lonnie Johnson, a New Orleans guitarist who seemed to push Armstrong toward new creative heights. Thanks in part to Johnson's strumming, "Hotter Than That" is "three minutes of daunting surprises," biographer Gary Giddins wrote in *Satchmo: The Genius of Louis Armstrong*, and the tune features some of the best horn playing and singing the jazzman had recorded to date.

## THE "UNHOLY THREE"

If the latter half of 1927 brought studio success, it also found Armstrong wanting for live work. He had left the Vendome in April, and by the summer, the Sunset had closed down, falling victim to frequent police raids. Figuring there was strength in numbers, Armstrong banded together with friends and former Stompers Earl Hines and Zutty Singleton—a pianist and drummer, respectively—and made a pact. Each member of the "Unholy Three," as the brotherhood was called, swore not to take a job unless the other two were also hired.

The three musicians also pooled together some money and opened their own South Side nightspot. Armstrong, Hines, and Singleton were great jazzmen, but their musical skills did not quite translate to business. The club failed, as did a second they tried soon after, and the musicians lost a substantial amount of money.

Their pact did not fare much better. While Hines was away in New York, Armstrong and Singleton again went to work for Dickerson, who was by this time leading a new band at the 4,000-capacity Savoy Ballroom. Hines was upset, but within a year, he would forgive his old pals and join them in the studio. In June 1928, the Unholy Three enlisted three members of Dickerson's Savoy ensemble and began recording the final batch of Hot Fives. The most widely known of these sides is "West End Blues," a performance many consider to be the finest Armstrong ever committed to wax.

## ARMSTRONG'S MASTERPIECES

Armstrong opens the tune with a nine-measure passage that accomplished jazz players still struggle to duplicate. During the final chorus—one that is completely different from the three that precede it—Armstrong starts simple, holding a B-flat note for four solid measures, then blasts off with a "stammering repetitive phrase that seems to float, completely unencumbered rhythmically, above the accompaniment," composer Gunther Schuller wrote in *Early Jazz: Its Roots and Musical Development.*

Perhaps more than any other recording Armstrong made in the late 1920s, "West End Blues" signaled the death of ensemble jazz—and the birth of the soloist. The trumpeter had been emphasizing solos for some time, and thanks to the addition of Hines, a musician who did for the piano what Armstrong had done for the trumpet, he reached a new creative pinnacle.

The two musicians knew as soon as they heard "West End Blues" that they had done something great. Before long, other musicians took notice. "Sometimes the record would make me so sad I'd cry up a storm," the great jazz singer Billie Holiday wrote in her autobiography. "Other times the same damn record would make me so happy." Collier wrote of the tune, "The piece is, indeed, Shakespearian: richly clothed, full of event, and rounded to a finish. All of Armstrong's strengths are at their peak: the warm golden tone, the knife-edged attack, the supreme confidence and control of his instrument."

Comprising five dozen sides—all of the Hot Fives, Hot Sevens, and records that, despite being credited to different bands, fall under their umbrella—Armstrong's output from 1925 to 1928 is what most jazz experts talk about when they discuss the genius of Louis Armstrong. Had he never recorded another tune, these tracks alone would have made him a legend.

Although Armstrong would, over the next four decades, achieve even greater commercial success, recasting himself as a movie star, TV personality, and best-selling pop artist, he never again played jazz as inventive or swinging. This was—and is—a source of great disappointment for purists, but it bears repeating that Armstrong never aspired to be simply a jazz musician. He wanted only to entertain, and in the years that followed, he realized his dream.

# 6

# The Jazzman Goes Pop

**By 1929, the Savoy Ballroom's** management was struggling to pay its musicians. Fortunately for Louis Armstrong, OKeh's recording director, Tommy Rockwell, had a plan, one that would alter the course of the trumpeter's career. Rockwell knew nothing about music—it was said he was hopelessly tone-deaf—but he knew show business. He was convinced Armstrong had the charisma needed to reach a mass audience. Eager to test this hunch (and make some money in the process), he invited the trumpeter to New York City for a recording session.

Rockwell decided Armstrong should be backed by pianist Leon Russell and his band, one of the more accomplished and authentic-sounding jazz outfits playing in New York. Russell's group featured several New Orleans natives, among them Pops Foster, a bassist Armstrong had worked with back in his riverboat days. Upon returning to the Big Apple, Armstrong joined

Russell and his men for a performance at Harlem's Savoy Ballroom. Intended as a rehearsal for the next day's recording session, the show had fans lining up around the block. Among those in attendance was King Oliver. It was likely the last time Oliver watched his former protégé perform. Years later, Armstrong recalled looking into the audience and seeing the elder musician cry.

After the Savoy show, a group of New York musicians threw Armstrong a banquet. The jazzmen ate and drank until well past midnight. At some point in the evening, Jack Condon, a white banjo player from Chicago, suggested the assembled jazz luminaries take their party into the recording studio. Rockwell gave Condon the go-ahead, and after having breakfast at 6:00 A.M., Armstrong arrived at the studio, a jug of whiskey in hand.

Armstrong's first racially mixed session yielded one cut, "Knockin' A Jug," a tune whose name speaks to that morning's partylike atmosphere. The song was nothing more than a series of blues solos, but it served as a warm-up for that afternoon's session, the one that had brought Armstrong to New York in the first place. Backed by Russell's nine-piece ensemble, Armstrong recorded two songs, starting with "I Can't Give You Anything But Love," the first of the big-band pop-style tunes that would become his stock and trade for the next two decades.

"I Can't Give You Anything But Love," from the long-running all-black Broadway show *Blackbirds of 1928*, was a popular tune at the time, but whereas previous renditions of the song had been cheery and hopeful, Rockwell instructed Armstrong to sing and play with a twinge of sadness. He did just that, using his unique phrasing and trumpet playing to completely transform what, in the hands of less imaginative musicians, had been a fairly standard pop ballad.

Although many jazz purists now claim "I Can't Give You Anything But Love" was the moment Armstrong forever turned his back on serious jazz, such criticisms were made by individuals who failed to understand the trumpeter's true nature. The song was simply another example of Armstrong moving out from behind the music stand and edging his way into the spotlight, where he had always wanted to be. Armstrong, who had no interest in playing for the pleasure of learned jazz scholars, saw nothing wrong with recording mainstream pop songs.

## ARMSTRONG ON BROADWAY

After the landmark Russell session, Armstrong returned briefly to Chicago. Rockwell telegrammed soon after with an offer to play in *Great Day*, a new Broadway musical set on a Southern plantation. Armstrong accepted, but he did not want to leave the Windy City without his friends in the Carroll Dickerson band. The musicians piled into four cars and drove east, buying food and gas with the money Rockwell had forwarded to Armstrong. Along the way, the jazzmen passed through a number of African-American communities and were heartened to discover just how popular Armstrong's records had become.

The musicians just barely made it to New York—the radiator in Armstrong's car broke as the caravan passed through Times Square. To make matters worse, the trumpeter had not told Rockwell he was bringing an entire band. *Great Day* did not need the whole Dickerson crew, but luckily, Rockwell was able to find the band work at the Audubon nightclub.

While his friends settled into their Audubon booking, Armstrong traveled to Philadelphia, where the *Great Day* rehearsals were taking place. Shortly after his arrival, he somehow ran afoul of musical director Robert Goetzl and, like many of the other black jazzmen hired for the production, was fired after a short time. Whatever the reason for his dismissal—race may have been a factor—Armstrong did not have to wait long for a second chance at Broadway. While he was in Philadelphia, the Dickerson group had landed a job at the Harlem nightspot Connie's Inn, then home of a popular all-black revue titled *Hot Chocolates*. A second version of the show was set to open on

Broadway, and Armstrong, ever the workhorse, signed on for both productions. He would play each night in the Broadway orchestra pit, take his bows, and then head uptown to Connie's, where he would do the show all over again.

In the summer of 1929, Armstrong recorded a version of "Ain't Misbehavin'," one of the show's more popular numbers. Once again, Armstrong gave a jazzy flourish to what was essentially a standard pop tune, reprising the formula he had established with "I Can't Give You Anything But Love." Over the next year or so, he continued recording in this style—and many of the songs he cut went on to become jazz standards.

A testament to his skill and innate sense of rhythm, Armstrong found a way to swing even nonswinging tunes, typically without much help from his sidemen. Armstrong's early big-band recordings lack the spirit of musical competitiveness and one-upmanship found on the best of his Hot Fives and Sevens. He was content to work with merely adequate backing musicians, men who would give what was required of them—nothing more, nothing less. Although it is possible Armstrong simply did not want to be overshadowed on these recordings, another explanation is that he wanted his records to be simple, straightforward, and melodic, qualities King Oliver had always emphasized with the Creole Jazz Band.

After *Hot Chocolates* closed, Connie Immerman, the owner of Connie's, fired Armstrong and the Dickerson band. More certain than ever he had a superstar on his hands, Rockwell urged Armstrong to leave the band and go it alone. Around the same time, Singleton took a job with another group, telling Armstrong that his decision to leave the ensemble was strictly a matter of business. Armstrong was furious, and the friends had a falling-out.

### DRUG ARREST

In July 1930, with his band now dissolved, Armstrong traveled to Los Angeles, where Rockwell had booked him at Culver

City's Cotton Club, an upscale establishment frequented by movie stars. The night before his debut, Armstrong cut what would be his final record with Lil, who, during a short period of reconciliation, had traveled with him to California. The pair backed the country singer Jimmie Rodgers on "Blue Yodel No. 9 (Standing on the Corner)," a tune that further showcased Armstrong's broad taste in music.

Armstrong worked for seven months at the Cotton Club. Although prohibition was still in effect, the local police allowed the club to serve alcohol to its rich and famous patrons. During this time, he performed with two bands: one led by Leon Elkins, the other by Les Hite. Highlights from the records he cut with both outfits during this period include "I'm A Ding Dong Daddy," another song featuring scat vocals, and "Shine," a tune Armstrong managed to make sound empowering, despite lyrics that are racially condescending by modern standards.

By this time, Armstrong had become a regular user of marijuana, a drug he discovered in 1928 and smoked daily for the rest of his life. ("Muggles," a song he cut that year, is a celebration of the substance.) Although arguably less destructive than alcohol or the harder drugs favored by many jazz greats—especially heroin—marijuana was nevertheless illegal. This proved problematic in November 1930, when Armstrong was arrested during one of his customary intermission smoke breaks. The Cotton Club's marquee trumpeter was likely set up by owners of a rival nightspot, and Armstrong was sentenced to 30 days in jail.

Fortunately, Armstrong had been caught smoking with Vic Berton, a jazz drummer whose boss at the Coconut Lounge had a well-connected brother named Tommy Lyman. Lyman seems to have called in favors: Following some shady dealings that likely involved local gangsters, the judge agreed to let off both Berton and Armstrong with suspended sentences. Armstrong served just nine days before he was allowed to leave California and take a job at Chicago's Showboat Theater.

## BAND ON THE RUN

The Showboat engagement had been booked by Johnny Collins, a mysterious East Coast gangster who, at some point that fall, had replaced Rockwell as Armstrong's manager. The trumpeter himself would later say he was never sure how Collins had acquired his contract.

One night in April 1931, after performing his set, Armstrong retired to his dressing room and came face to face with Frankie Foster, an armed gangster from New York. Foster told Armstrong he had better get on a train for the Big Apple, as he was scheduled to perform there the next evening. The trumpeter corrected him, insisting his gig was in Chicago, to which Foster responded by cocking his weapon and leading Armstrong outside to a pay phone. After Foster handed Armstrong the receiver, someone on the other end—Immerman, probably—further tried to intimidate the musician into heading back east.

As Armstrong would learn, his management transition had not been a smooth one. Rockwell and Collins were engaged in a battle over his contract. The dispute would ultimately be settled in court, but at the time, Armstrong had every reason to fear for his life. The mafia controlled the music business in those days. Even though Armstrong was a successful entertainer capable of making club owners great sums of money, he was just a pawn in a dangerous game. As far as Collins could tell, there was only one solution: He and Armstrong hightailed it out of Chicago, staging an impromptu tour that included a prolonged stay in New Orleans.

Armstrong had not been to his hometown since the day he left to join King Oliver in Chicago. As his train pulled into the station, he received a hero's welcome, complete with balloons, marching bands, and thousands of cheering fans. Collins had booked Armstrong at the all-white Suburban Gardens, and despite an unfortunate opening-night incident—a radio announcer referred to him with a racial slur—the engagement lasted three months.

While in the Big Easy, Armstrong was generous with his time and money. He bought radios for the Colored Waif's Home and sponsored a youth baseball team, furnishing the players with crisp new uniforms. Armstrong had been traveling without Lil since Los Angeles, and during this time, the couple legally separated, paving the way for a divorce that would follow in 1938.

Because of the Rockwell-Collins contract situation, Armstrong spent the months after his New Orleans residency zigzagging across the country, avoiding New York and Chicago at all costs. Race relations being what they then were, the musician was often treated poorly, even in cities where he was drawing large audiences. "Why, do you know I played ninety-nine *million* hotels I couldn't stay at? And if I had friends blowing at some all-white nightclub or hotel I couldn't get in to see 'em—or them to see me," he said, as quoted in *Warning, Writer at Work*, a collection of writings by Larry L. King.

In Memphis, Collins's wife, a white woman, defied a bus dispatcher who ordered Armstrong and his entourage to trade their large, comfortable bus for a smaller one. The bus company called the police, and Armstrong, simply by virtue of traveling with a white woman—which was illegal in the South at the time—found himself in danger of serving jail time. He escaped this fate by agreeing to play a benefit concert for the local police. The officers may have strong-armed the musician into raising money for their department, but Armstrong was at least able to get off a decent parting shot. During the concert, he dedicated "(I'll Be Glad When You're Dead) You Rascal You" to the Memphis Police Department.

In late 1931, Armstrong finally returned to Chicago, where he cut his final sides for OKeh. The band he led was considerably less polished than the Cotton Club ensemble he had last recorded with, but the sessions nevertheless produced a number of tunes that would become Armstrong hallmarks, including "Sleepytime Down South," his theme song. Many of Armstrong's songs from this era were ballads, and on such selections as "Stardust," his vocal phrasing was nearly as innovative as his earlier trumpet playing had been. He drew influence from his friend Bing Crosby, who was by this time a major star, and placed greater emphasis on his singing.

## LONDON CALLING

At this stage in his career, Armstrong's records were selling well, and he was earning a respectable $1,000 per tune. Just as the trumpeter was becoming more famous across the United States, Collins received an offer to book his client in London. Armstrong, accompanied by Alpha, left for England in July 1932. Although he was not the first American jazz musician to cross the pond—both Sidney Bechet and the Original Dixieland Jazz Band had brought hot music to Great Britain nearly 15 years earlier—he was the first to arrive in Europe with any semblance of preexisting fame. OKeh had, by this time, issued European pressings of his recordings, and British musicians were already trying to replicate his style.

It was upon arriving in London that Armstrong may have received his most famous nickname. According to legend, Perry Mathison Brooks, the editor of the English music magazine *Melody Maker*, was among those on hand to greet the jazzman as he came ashore, and he did so by exclaiming, "Hello, Satchmo!" At least that is how Armstrong heard it. Brooks probably referred to him as "Satchelmouth"—a tag Armstrong had acquired as a boy, when friends would tease him about his large mouth—but failed to enunciate it completely. The name stuck, and Armstrong was forevermore known as Satchmo, or Satch for short.

Due to restrictions set by England's Department of Labour, foreign musicians were not allowed to play nightclubs or

Louis Armstrong and Alpha Smith, who later became his third wife, wait on a train platform with a pet terrier in London, England, in the autumn of 1933. It was during his enormously successful tour in Great Britain that he earned his nickname, Satchmo.

cabarets. This left Armstrong with little choice but to perform at the London Palladium, a large theater famous for hosting vaudeville acts. The trumpeter debuted at the Palladium on July 18, 1932, and if his band—composed of musicians he had just met—was not exactly up to the task, he still managed to impress the country's small cadre of serious jazz critics.

Unfortunately, he did not fare as well with general audiences or the mainstream press. Even some of England's budding jazz

## What's in a Name?

In his lifetime, Louis Armstrong was called many things. As a boy, his large mouth earned him such nicknames as Dippermouth, Gatemouth, and Satchelmouth—the tag that, thanks to a British journalist's accent, eventually morphed into Satchmo, then Satch for short. Armstrong often referred to himself as "Pops," a tag he also used when addressing others, and he frequently signed his letters "your boy."

Given this plethora of nicknames, it is perhaps not surprising that the trumpeter's real name has long been a point of controversy. Early biographies of the jazzman stated his full name as Daniel Louis Armstrong, although birth records have since shown that Daniel was not, as the trumpeter himself maintained, part of his name. Then, there's the question of his first name: Was it pronounced "Loo-is" or "Loo-ee"?

Those who argue for the former cite as their prime example the 1964 hit "Hello, Dolly!" in which Armstrong clearly sings, "This is Louisss, Dolly," as if to emphasize the "s" sound at the end of his name. Those in the "Loo-is" camp also point out that Armstrong was not French, and that it would not have made sense for him to pronounce his name Louie. What's more, it has been said that his mother, the one responsible for naming him, always used Louis.

Complicating matters is the fact that two of Armstrong's wives called him both Louis and Louie. Also, in 1933, he recorded a song called "Laughin' Louie," a comic tune in which he describes waking up each day and chuckling at the pictures of himself that hang on his wall. "That's why they call me Laughin' Louie," he sings. Other musicians seemed to have preferred that pronunciation, and on the 1957 recording "A Fine Romance," duet partner Ella Fitzgerald sings, "You know, Louie, we don't have half the thrills that the march of time has."

musicians scoffed at his live show, struggling to reconcile the masterful sounds of his records with the man they saw onstage: an intense performer who would make faces and growl into the microphone, all the while sweating profusely. Some writers called his act "savage" and "barbaric"—words that revealed more about their racist attitudes than their knowledge of jazz.

That said, Armstrong continued to stage concerts throughout England, and press coverage followed wherever he went. He kept many of the clippings from that tour, adding them to the scrapbook he maintained throughout his life.

## TROUBLE ON THE HOME FRONT

By November, after he wrapped his English tour and sailed back to New York, Armstrong had become more famous in Europe than he was in the United States. At home, he received little coverage in major newspapers and magazines. Presumably lacking a better job offer, he remained in the Big Apple for a time and played in a poorly received revival of *Hot Chocolates*. When the show closed, he teamed up with a band led by Chick Webb and made his first in a series of unmemorable recordings for his new label, Victor.

Armstrong ended 1932 with a New Year's Eve show in Baltimore, where years of constant touring and incorrect technique finally caught up with him: He split his lip onstage. With blood gushing from his mouth, he was forced to bid the crowd an early goodnight. He rested his lips—or "chops," as he called them—for a few weeks before returning to Chicago to record with a new band. On January 26, he cut six sides, two of which, "I Gotta Right to Sing the Blues" and "I've Got the World on a String," are regarded as rare highlights of his Victor recording period.

During this time, Armstrong and his new group began playing shows throughout the Midwest. Although he was friendly with his sidemen, he mostly kept to himself, retreating to his bus or dressing room after shows and typing letters to friends, one of his favorite hobbies. Onstage, of course, he was more outgoing, and in towns where he was not yet well known, he would strain to thrill his audiences, sometimes blowing upward of 250 high-C notes in a row.

Serious jazz fans decried these displays of showmanship, insisting Armstrong was above such crass gimmickry, but if the trumpeter was aware of such criticism, it is doubtful he paid it much mind. Fans loved to hear his crisp, powerful playing, and that was precisely what he was going to give them.

One night, before a performance in Philadelphia, Armstrong had another run-in with gangsters. Fearing the men would be waiting for him in his dressing room after the show, he ducked out a stage door after finishing his set and ran to the nearest police station. Soon after, he called Collins and suggested they

## DID YOU KNOW?

Louis Armstrong was nearly as prolific a writer as he was a musician. In addition to his two autobiographies—the heavily ghostwritten 1936 volume *Swing That Music*, often referred to as the first autobiography of a jazz musician, and his 1954 memoir, *Satchmo: My Life in New Orleans*, which covers his life up until 1922—Satchmo penned dozens of magazine articles. His work appeared in such wide-ranging publications as *Holiday*, the *Harlem Tattler*, and the *New York Times Book Review*. In 1954, he wrote a piece for *Ebony* titled "Why I Like Dark Women." In his spare time, he often dashed off letters to friends, sometimes using a typewriter, other times with green pens and yellow paper. He wrote much like he spoke, using colorful, comical language. "He was unschooled in spelling and grammar, but he had an ear for language and could express himself with enviable clarity in trim, speechlike cadences," Giddins wrote in *Satchmo: The Genius of Louis Armstrong*. Many of Armstrong's personal writings were collected in 1999's *Louis Armstrong, In His Own Words*. He is rumored to have completed a follow-up to *Satchmo: My Life in New Orleans*, which he intended to have published after his death, but the manuscript has never been found.

get out of town—fast. This time, however, a U.S. tour would not be good enough. It would have to be Europe.

On the subsequent boat ride to England, Armstrong and Collins got into an argument about what songs Satchmo should play during his upcoming tour. Collins was drunk and used a racial slur in the heat of the moment. Had there not already been tension between the two men, their partnership might have survived the incident. Unfortunately, Collins had been causing problems for some time. He often clashed with concert promoters, which gave Armstrong unnecessary head-aches, and his mob connections had more than once put the musician's life at risk.

English music magazines ran stories about their falling-out—further proof of how famous Armstrong was over-seas—and shortly after arriving in London, the musician fired his manager.

## VICTORY IN EUROPE

Armstrong fared well on his own, at least for a while, win-ning accolades even without proper management. During a command performance for King George V, he declared, "This one's for you, Rex," just before launching into "You Ras-cal You." The audience must have been more charmed than aghast, as Armstrong left with a gold trumpet, compliments of the king.

After finishing his English tour, Armstrong traveled to Denmark, where the popularity of his records had already made him a major star. Thousands of fans greeted him as his train pulled into Copenhagen. While he was in the country, he recorded three songs for a film about a Dutch radio station. At this point in his career, Armstrong had already adopted many of his trademark stage mannerisms, and the footage shows him clutching a white handkerchief and dancing along with the music.

In May 1934, after performing shows across Scandinavia and making a return trip to England, Armstrong headed to Paris for a rare breather. The vacation was a matter of necessity: He had again split his lip at a recent London concert and decided to rest his aching chops. Throughout the spring and summer, he visited Parisian jazz clubs and mingled with French musicians, among them the gypsy guitarist Django Reinhardt, a longtime Armstrong admirer.

The trumpeter did not resume playing until November, when he went into a studio to record several songs for the Brunswick label. Days later, he made his French concert debut, performing alongside the Parisian musicians who had backed him on his recent recording session. The show was a huge success—Armstrong later wrote about going back onstage after having changed into his bathrobe in order to satisfy fans' demands for multiple encores. Armstrong's European tour continued until he again split his lip, this time in Turin, Italy. The injured jazzman promptly returned home to Chicago, where, on doctor's orders, he took a six-month break.

## NEW MANAGER, NEW DIRECTION

In addition to serious health concerns—according to fellow trumpeter Arthur Briggs, Armstrong's lips were, by this time, "as hard as a piece of wood"—Louis soon found himself grappling with legal troubles. Collins was readying a breach-of-contract suit, and Lil, having failed to receive $6,000 in "maintenance" money she was owed under the terms of their separation, was threatening legal action of her own.

For help, Armstrong turned to Joe Glaser, the nightclub manager and small-time gangster he had met years earlier at the Sunset Café. A Chicago native, Glaser was notoriously brash, controlling, and foul-mouthed. He had overseen Al Capone's South Side nightspots and brothels in the 1920s and had managed prizefighters, among other business dealings. Some claimed he had also served time for murder. Even if that rumor was untrue, the fact remained that Glaser was a cut-throat businessman—a shrewd schemer who would stop at nothing to succeed. He was, in other words, exactly the kind of manager Armstrong needed, and the two formed a partnership that would last until Glaser's death in 1969.

Although Armstrong and Glaser were never exactly friends—they rarely socialized and spoke more often on the phone than in person—they seemed to share a great fondness and admiration for each other. From the beginning, Glaser believed that Armstrong had the talent to be a superstar and made managing the trumpeter's career his top priority. Like King Oliver before him, Glaser was a surrogate father to Armstrong—a strong older man whose approval the musician craved.

Indeed, the jazzman always referred to him as "Mr. Glaser," and on occasions when people dared question his manager's character, the typically easygoing Armstrong would rush to his defense, raising his voice in anger. Toward the end of his life, as Armstrong lay in a hospital bed revising his autobiography, he wrote, "I dedicate this book/ to my manager and pal/ Mr. Joe Glaser/ The best friend/ that I've ever had,/ May the Lord Bless him/ Watch over him always/ His boy and disciple who loved him/ dearly./ Louis/ Satchmo/ Armstrong."

At this point in his career, Armstrong was earning good money, both as a recording artist and a touring artist, but he had little interest in amassing a fortune. When he hired Glaser, he asked that his new manager take complete control of his business affairs. Glaser was to book Armstrong's tours, pay his band members, file his tax returns, and generally handle anything that might distract him from blowing his horn. For his troubles, Glaser was to keep all of the profit, minus the $1,000 Armstrong asked for each week.

The two later amended their agreement and settled on a 50–50 split. Even then, some accused Glaser of taking advantage of his star client and pocketing more than his share.

Whatever the case, Armstrong seems to have been content with their arrangement. With each other's help, both men became millionaires. Even if Armstrong, the talent in their operation, may have been entitled to a greater percentage of the profits, he was living a life far beyond his wildest dreams. He thought it unnecessary to ask for more money. As he saw it, he owed much of his success to Glaser's business savvy.

It did not take long for Glaser to start earning his lofty pay. Immediately after taking charge of Armstrong's career, he settled Armstrong's legal troubles with Collins and Lil, paying the former the modern-day equivalent of $73,000. With his lip somewhat healed and his personal affairs finally in order, Armstrong recommitted himself to his true passion: entertaining.

## CROSSOVER STAR

Glaser, like Rockwell, recognized Armstrong's potential for mainstream success. He convinced the jazzman to tone down the showy trumpet playing that had contributed to his lip injury and to concentrate more on being an entertainer, a smiling song-and-dance man who would appeal to blacks and whites alike. Armstrong was happy to oblige—after all, Glaser's show-business philosophy was very much in line with his own. In subsequent concerts and recording sessions, he took to heart what had been his manager's advice: "Play and sing pretty. Give the people a show."

Although his voice remained raspy, Armstrong smoothed his delivery some because he thought it would make his music more palatable to white listeners. Whatever the reason, the improved delivery worked—before long, jazz fanatics and record-collecting college students were not the only ones lining up for Satch's concerts.

In 1936, with his celebrity on the rise, Armstrong made his Hollywood feature debut, starring with Bing Crosby in *Pennies from Heaven*. In doing so, he became the first black entertainer to earn top billing in a major studio picture. Crosby, a coproducer on the project, had insisted that Armstrong appear in the film, and the two share several comedic scenes. Although "Skeleton in the Closet," Armstrong's big musical number, is yet another example of a song that appears racist to modern audiences, its style of comedy was fairly common for the time. *Pennies from Heaven* did well at the box office, and Armstrong earned complimentary reviews. He approached his film work with the same dedication and professionalism he did his music; in 1937, he was among the founders of the Negro Actors Guild.

Other movies followed, and although Armstrong usually played lovable, dim-witted characters—"Uncle Tom" types, as some critics would insist—he proved a natural actor and comedian. Even when the material was second-rate, he had an undeniable screen presence critics admired. As movie roles added to his fame, major publications that had once ignored him suddenly began running stories. In all, Armstrong would make more than 30 films and would work with such diverse screen legends as Mae West, Barbra Streisand, Jack Benny, and Ronald Reagan.

Armstrong also kept busy on the music front, signing a contract with Decca Records. The label's founder, Jack Kapp, was a savvy marketer whose approach to the music business was best summed up by a sign posted in his studio: "Where's the melody?" Kapp had previously worked with Crosby, urging him to scale back his jazzy scat singing and croon the kinds of sweet pop tunes that would sell large quantities of records. The approach worked—for years, Crosby was a fixture at the top of the charts—and Kapp aimed to take a similar tact with Armstrong.

Over the next six years, Kapp encouraged Armstrong to stray further from his jazz and blues roots. A devout lover of melody, the part of a song Oliver had taught him to prize most, Armstrong agreed to cut novelty tunes, gospel numbers, Hawaiian folk songs—anything Decca's executives thought the public would buy. If Armstrong sometimes deserved better material, he nevertheless gave his all to every session, using his immense talent to render even the most trite of songs.

In the summer of 1937, Armstrong added "radio star" to his list of accomplishments, becoming the first African-American entertainer to host a national variety program. The opportunity came about when popular NBC personality Rudy Vallée took a three-month vacation and tapped Armstrong to fill in over the summer. *Harlem*, as Armstrong's program was called, featured comedy skits and musical numbers. Since 1935, Armstrong had been leading a new band, the Leon Russell group he had formerly worked with in New York. With a lineup that included several New Orleans musicians, including drummer Paul Barbarin and bassist Pops Foster, Russell's outfit provided suitably swinging accompaniment, both on *Harlem* and Armstrong's best Decca sides.

## King of Swing? Not Quite.

From the mid-1930s until the end of World War II, a form of big-band jazz known as "swing" enjoyed massive popularity, making superstars of such bandleaders as Duke Ellington, Count Basie, Benny Goodman, Glenn Miller, and Tommy Dorsey. Although swing had evolved out of the dance-band music of the 1920s, its sprightly rhythms and tight ensemble playing—notable for the presence of saxophones—appealed to teenage fans too young to have heard the New Orleans-style jazz that had preceded it.

Although Armstrong fronted a big band throughout the Swing Era, he and his sidemen were not quite in step with the times. "Swing bands were essentially dance orchestras designed for ballrooms, although they frequently played theaters," Collier writes in *Louis Armstrong: An American Genius*. "Armstrong was really a vaudevillian playing theatrical shows."

The difference is subtle, but worth pointing out. Whereas the era's bandleaders staffed their orchestras with multiple skilled soloists, ensuring that they themselves were not the only ones capable of stepping out front and wowing the audience, Armstrong generally worked with average players—musicians who soloed only when Satchmo needed a breather.

Among Armstrong's finer Decca recordings was his 1938 rendition of "When the Saints Go Marching In." His was the first-ever swinging version of the spiritual number, and thanks to his stellar performance, the tune went on to become a jazz standard. The same year Armstrong cut "Saints," Glaser booked him at New York's Cotton Club, where he met Lucille Wilson, the woman who was to become his fourth and final wife. Lucille was an unassuming middle-class chorus girl from Queens. She sold homemade cookies to members of the band and chorus before each show, using the extra money to help support her family, which had fallen on hard times during the Great Depression. A smitten Armstrong would sometimes buy up her entire stock.

Although Armstrong had just recently married Alpha, their relationship was already in trouble. If Alpha had originally seemed easygoing and unpretentious—the antidote to Lil and

The best swing bands also featured innovative arrangements. For example, such genre classics as Glenn Miller's "In the Mood" hinged on an ensemble's ability to come together and, in compelling fashion, power through catchy melodies. Again, in the case of Armstrong's big bands, the other musicians were largely hired hands there to serve Satchmo.

As such, many young fans growing up in the Swing Era viewed Armstrong as slightly out of fashion. In 1944, Satchmo's band failed to place on *Down Beat*'s year-end best-of list, and for a time, Armstrong fared nearly as poorly on the annual list of notable trumpeters, polling behind younger, less-gifted horn players.

After World War II, changing public tastes and high musicians' salaries spelled the end of swing. The next decade would see the rise of superstar vocalists, and although Armstrong would never challenge such heartthrobs as Frank Sinatra for control of the youth market, he managed to change with the times. Initially reluctant to break up his big band, Armstrong eventually formed the All-Stars, a sextet that played neither swing nor 1920s-style Dixieland, but rather an audience-friendly mix of jazz and pop.

her highfalutin ways—she had grown increasingly materialistic and difficult to please. Armstrong lavished her with jewels and furs, but as he would later write, his gifts were never enough. "We had some real spats," he wrote in a 1954 piece for *Ebony*. "She'd get to drinking and grab that big pocketbook of hers and hit me in my chops with it."

The problems had started even before Armstrong married Alpha, and at one point, he begged Lil not to divorce him. Alpha was pushing for a wedding ring, but as long as he was legally married, he could continue stringing her along and postpone another walk down the aisle. Lil refused to help out, and less than two weeks after the divorce was finalized, Armstrong made Alpha his third wife. The marriage lasted four years, during which time Armstrong saw Lucille on the sly, taking her out whenever he was in New York.

## REMEMBERING THE OLD DAYS

In the late 1930s, as the big-band sound favored by Armstrong and his ensemble remained en vogue, a subset of fans and record collectors began rediscovering the small-ensemble "hot" jazz of the previous decade. Decca caught wind of the trend, and in 1940, Kapp commissioned a session that reunited Armstrong with Zutty Singleton and Sidney Bechet, his onetime musical sparring partner.

Recording such tunes as "2:19 Blues" and "Coal Cart Blues," Armstrong and Bechet played well together but struggled to recapture the old magic. Bechet later claimed that Armstrong tried too hard to turn each of the Decca songs into one of their classic 1920s-era duels. If that was the case, Armstrong may have been overcompensating after years of playing undemanding material. Whatever the reason, the sides were disappointing. Many fans of Dixieland, as original New Orleans-style jazz was by now being called, realized they were better off buying Columbia Records' Hot Five reissues, released around the same time.

In April 1938, just as Dixieland was coming back in fashion, one of the genre's pioneers, King Oliver, died. Armstrong had last seen his former mentor in Savannah, Georgia, where Oliver spent the final years of his life living in poverty and obscurity. Oliver had been reduced to running a produce stand. As Armstrong and his men passed through town on one of their tours, they gave him what money they had—a final tribute to the once-great horn player.

### BIG-BAND TOURS

With the occasional lineup change—Glaser demoted Russell from musical director to pianist, replacing him with Joe Garland, composer of the swing classic "In the Mood"—Armstrong and his band spent the next few years on the road. They specialized in one-nighters in cities across the country, and Alpha, still Armstrong's wife, traveled with the band, ironing the white handkerchiefs her husband would famously use to mop his brow onstage.

Alpha's days of doing Armstrong's laundry were numbered, however. On October 2, 1942, the couple finally divorced, paving the way for Armstrong to marry Lucille, which he did just 10 days later. After his troubles with Lil and Alpha, Armstrong was happy to have finally found a woman with a similar outlook on life. "In fact it dawned on me—it seemed to me that Lucille was the ideal girl for me," he wrote in a letter reprinted in *Louis Armstrong, In His Own Words*. "In fact our lives were practically the same. Good Common Sense—great observers (not for any particular reason) but were not particular about phony people, etc.—what we *didn't* have we *did* without."

Lucille spent her first eight months as Mrs. Armstrong touring with the band. She soon realized, however, that she did not share her husband's taste for the road. In the spring of 1943, she scraped together some money and put a down payment on a house in the Corona section of Queens, New York. Armstrong was dubious about settling down—he had,

In 1943, Louis Armstrong's fourth wife, Lucille, purchased and decorated a home for the couple in Queens, New York. Here, Louis Armstrong's den in the home is shown, where he used his tape decks to record hours and hours of music and conversations.

after all, been in a state of perpetual motion since leaving New Orleans two decades earlier—but he decided to give it a chance. On the night he was to first see his new home, he had a taxi driver wait outside, just in case he did not like the place and wanted to leave. As it happened, no hasty retreat was necessary. Armstrong not only fell in love with the house, but he invited the driver in for dinner.

Although Armstrong remained on the road for much of the next two decades, spending little time in Corona, he enjoyed having a place he could call home. In the late 1960s, as his touring pace finally began to slow, he delighted in getting to know the neighborhood children and spending time in his office, where, using reel-to-reel tapes, he obsessively archived and catalogued his recordings, TV appearances, radio broadcasts, and other performances. Also included in his colossal collection of tapes—stored in hand-decorated boxes—were favorite records by other artists, snatches of party chatter and small talk with friends, radio coverage of Martin Luther King Jr.'s funeral, and various other events, conversations, and pieces of music he saw fit to record.

By the late 1940s, big-band music had started to fall from fashion. Some of the genre's giants, such as Tommy Dorsey and Benny Goodman, were disbanding their groups, paving the way for an era of popular music in which singers, not instrumentalists, would reign supreme. At the same time, a new generation of radical musicians in the jazz world was ushering in the "bebop" era. With its angular, avant-garde instrumental leads and wild rhythms, bebop marked a major departure from the hot jazz and swing that had preceded it. Armstrong was suspicious of this new sound. Although he dabbled in the style, cutting the vaguely bebop-inspired Decca sides "Snafu" and "Jodie Man," he was seen by many young jazz fans as old-fashioned and out of touch.

These two trends—the death of big band and birth of bebop—left Armstrong in a strange position. He could not compete with renegade bop saxophonist Charlie Parker for the youth audience—the kids in Harlem were well beyond tuxes and white handkerchiefs—nor could he go on touring with his 18-piece ensemble, even though he was still playing to full houses and earning the applause he desired more than anything.

In order to remain relevant, Armstrong was going to have to make some changes.

# 7

# Louis the All-Star

**The series of events that led** to Louis Armstrong abandoning big-band music began with *New Orleans*, a 1947 film that, though riddled with historical inaccuracies and racially insensitive character portrayals (the great singer Billie Holiday played a maid), recounts the story of early jazz. *New Orleans* was made at a time when enthusiasm for bebop and nostalgia for Dixieland were beginning to earn jazz the respect it had long been denied. Even if Hollywood got the story of jazz completely wrong, it at least deemed it a story worth telling.

Producers tapped Armstrong, appropriately enough, to score the film's honky-tonk scenes. Instead of playing classic Dixieland or the big-band style he had favored in recent years, the jazz veteran aimed for something in between. The small group he led included Big Easy alumni Kid Ory and Zutty Singleton, and it played updated versions of early jazz classics, such as "Basin Street Blues."

**Billie Holiday is shown singing in the only movie she made, *New Orleans*, which was released in 1947. Holiday, who was cast as a maid, was Louis Armstrong's girlfriend in the film. In her autobiography, *Lady Sings The Blues*, she bitterly condemned her experiences in Hollywood.**

Leonard Feather, who produced the *New Orleans* sessions, liked the sound, and he came up with the idea of having Armstrong lead a small ensemble at Carnegie Hall. It was to be the trumpeter's first concert at the famed New York City venue, and although Armstrong refused to do a full performance without his band—he was, as always, loyal to his sidemen—he agreed to open the show leading a pared-down sextet.

## SMALLER IS BETTER

On May 17, 1947, some three months after his Carnegie Hall performance, Armstrong played one of the most important concerts of his life—one that reaffirmed his relevance and set the stage for the next phase in his career. That night, he led a sextet staffed with expert jazz soloists, among them Jack Teagarden, the trombone ace with whom he had recorded nearly two decades earlier; drummers Sid Catlett and George Wettling; and pianist Dick Carey. According to those who attended the Town Hall concert, Armstrong appeared relaxed and rejuvenated. If he played the occasional high-C note, he did not go out of his way to overwhelm concertgoers with displays of trumpet fireworks.

As praise rolled in for Armstrong's Town Hall show, Glaser snapped into action, signing Teagarden to a contract and firing the big band Armstrong had led for more than a decade. For Glaser, the move was purely financial. If he had thought Armstrong could have made more money with the pop-oriented big band, he would have kept that ensemble on the road. The times had changed, however, and Glaser knew his marquee client needed to change with them. For the remainder of his career, Satch would lead a small ensemble, a rotating cast known as the All-Stars.

On August 13, 1947, Louis Armstrong and his new sextet—not yet christened the All-Stars—debuted at Billy Berg's Vine Street, the hip Hollywood nightclub where, two years earlier, bebop jazzmen Dizzy Gillespie and Charlie Parker had played their first West Coast shows. Armstrong and the crew—Teagarden, Catlett, and Cary from the Town Hall band, plus clarinetist Barney Bigard and singer Velma Middleton—took the stage after just two days of rehearsal. "I don't need no rehearsals," Armstrong was quoted as saying in *Time.* "I don't go through that and never will. All these cats I'm playing with can blow. We don't need no arrangements. . . . I say follow me, and you got the best arrangement you ever heard."

The show was generally well received, both by the press and by various entertainers—bandleader Benny Goodman and acclaimed songwriter Johnny Mercer, among them—on hand for the event. Glaser had been hesitant about announcing the demise of Armstrong's big band, but the success of the Vine Street performance erased his doubts. He was suddenly able to book the band for up to $4,000 per week, and Armstrong continued to command top dollar until the end of his life.

Glaser wasted no time capitalizing on Armstrong's heightened profile. He sent the band on an eastward trek, booking two night stands all the way from Los Angeles to Boston. From 1947 to 1951, Glaser continued to work the band hard; in that four-year period, Armstrong and the All-Stars made two European tours and traveled the United States no fewer than 10 times. While Satchmo's sidemen sometimes complained about the hectic schedule, Glaser did his best to keep up morale. The musicians earned good salaries, always had valets to take them from their hotels to the gigs, and could count on hot meals and freshly laundered suits. Armstrong, who lived to tour, was the least likely to complain; he believed playing frequently was crucial to maintaining the health of his chops.

By design, the All-Stars were a mixed-race ensemble. Glaser insisted on a diverse lineup, believing it would endear the band to middle-class whites. In the Town Hall version of the band, Catlett had been the only black member other than Armstrong. At the end of 1947, the reconfigured group was all black, except for Teagarden. During tours of the South, the white trombonist was forced to stay in a separate hotel. Armstrong shrugged off this unfortunate fact of life and remained upbeat. The only place he refused to play was Memphis, where he was not even allowed to share a stage with Teagarden.

## ON THE ROAD

As the All-Stars gained and lost members, Armstrong never concerned himself with hiring and firing musicians. This was another part of the operation he left in Glaser's hands. Although he expected his sidemen to be solid professionals capable of hitting the right notes, he had no interest in working with showboating glory hounds. Armstrong was a warm, friendly man, but this was his show. He was not going to be upstaged.

As months turned into years, Armstrong and the All-Stars developed a fairly consistent repertoire, opening each show with "Indiana" and closing with "When It's Sleepy Time Down South." The group rarely dabbled in Armstrong's Hot Five–era output, but even when it did, it stopped short of doing a Dixieland revival show. Just as he had done with the *New Orleans* score, Armstrong blended 1920s jazz with more modern sounds, creating a style of music that was beyond easy categorization. If Armstrong played the same solos every night, he nevertheless aimed to give fans a good show. He let his bandmates play their own solos and sang flirty duets with Middleton, a charming, overweight woman who would perform splits onstage.

### MULTIMEDIA SUPERSTAR

In 1948, Armstrong began his conquest of another medium: television. He and the All-Stars appeared on the variety show *Talk of the Town*, a program later renamed *The Ed Sullivan Show*, in honor of its host. The show became a Sunday night institution, airing until 1971, and throughout its run, Armstrong was one of Sullivan's regular guests.

## IN HIS OWN WORDS…

Despite his prodigious talents, Louis Armstrong tended to be a humble man. As he once explained to fellow musicians Bix Beiderbecke and Wingy Manone, as recounted in the book *Bix: Man & Legend*, his approach to playing solos was less complicated than it may have seemed. In order to keep from repeating himself, he said, he stuck with a simple formula: "Well, I tell you . . . the first chorus I plays the melody. The second chorus I plays the melody round the melody, and the third chorus I routines."

In February 1949, Armstrong returned to New Orleans and served as King of the Zulus in the city's annual Mardi Gras parade. Accepting the honor meant having to wear blackface makeup—the signature look of minstrel-show performers—and a grass skirt. Although this was yet another instance where critics accused him of playing along with racist stereotypes, Armstrong was genuinely honored to have been elected king. The Zulus, a group composed of working-class blacks, had been staging Mardi Gras parades for decades, typically choosing their kings and queens from their own humble ranks. That they would pick Armstrong—a wealthy celebrity who had left the Big Easy as a young man and never cared to return—was a testament to the respect they felt for Satchmo. The trumpeter donned his costume and rode his float with pride.

That same year, Armstrong made the cover of *Time*. The accompanying story told of the jazzman's early days and emphasized his newfound status as a major entertainer. He had gone from being a steady concert draw and fairly famous musician to a full-fledged star. From TV to movies, newspapers to radio, Satchmo was everywhere in the late 1940s. Even those with no interest in jazz knew his name.

## TRIBUTES

In the meantime, Armstrong continued recording for Decca. Producer Milt Gabler, like label-founder Kapp, was a firm believer in accessible pop, a style of music Armstrong was, as always, happy to deliver. Backed more often by studio musicians than his All-Stars, Armstrong spent the late 1940s and the 1950s covering current chart hits, trying his hand at everything from Hank Williams's country weeper "Your Cheating Heart" to the French ballad "La Vie en Rose."

In 1950, the American jazz magazine *Down Beat* marked what was believed to be Armstrong's fiftieth birthday with a special tribute issue. Two years later, Armstrong placed first in the

Louis Armstrong appeared on the cover of *Time* in February 1949. Since the 1920s, he had gone from being a popular trumpet player to one of the most recognizable musicians in the world. Even people without any interest in jazz knew who Satchmo was.

magazine's reader's poll of the "most important musical figure of all time," edging out the likes of Duke Ellington, who came in second, and Johann Sebastian Bach, who placed seventh.

In 1954, Armstrong published his second book, *Satchmo: My Life in New Orleans*, a memoir covering his early years. *Satchmo* followed the much-maligned *Horn of Plenty*, a biography written by Armstrong's friend Robert Goffin. Despite using an original Armstrong manuscript as his source material, Goffin turned the story of the trumpeter's life into what critics dubbed an overly sentimental, muddled mess. Armstrong's own memoir, by contrast, was accurate and amusing. The book ends with Armstrong taking the stage with King Oliver at Chicago's Lincoln Gardens, the most important moment of his young life. Some have speculated that Glaser ordered Armstrong to end his story in 1922, lest he invite trouble with tales of the marijuana use and mob altercations that colored his 1930s and 1940s adventures.

Even if it is incomplete—Armstrong was rumored to have been working on a second volume, though it has never surfaced—*Satchmo* is a dynamic story told in the jazzman's own voice. His editors may have fixed the musician's spelling and grammar, but they did little to alter his unique way with words. The book is filled with the kinds of colorful quips and descriptions he often used, whether speaking or writing.

## CHART SUCCESS

Although his place in musical history was secure, Armstrong was not finished making hit records. In 1956, his recording of "Blueberry Hill," cut seven years earlier, reached number 29 on the *Billboard* singles chart. Later that year, he achieved an even higher chart placement, reaching the top 20 with "Mack the Knife," a song from Bertolt Brecht and Kurt Weil's show *The Threepenny Opera*. The rock 'n' roll-era performers Fats Domino and Bobby Darin also had big hits with "Blueberry Hill" and "Mack the Knife," respectively, proving that even if

Armstrong was somewhat old-fashioned, his tastes were not totally out of step with the times.

Although singles had long been the dominant form of recorded music, the long-playing record, or LP, was becoming ever more popular by the 1950s. After Columbia Records had begun collecting Armstrong's early OKeh sides and issuing its *Louis Armstrong Story* LPs—compilations that sold well but earned Satchmo no money—label producer George Avakian set out to record new music with Armstrong. Avakian, who felt that Decca had led the trumpeter astray, came up with the idea of doing an album's worth of blues songs written by W.C. Handy, the so-called "father of the blues."

Glaser was not immediately sold on the idea. He saw nothing wrong with Decca's pop-centric handling of Armstrong's career. After Columbia's president agreed to pay Armstrong a one-percent royalty on the OKeh reissues, Glaser gave his approval. During sessions for what would become known as *Louis Armstrong Plays W.C. Handy*, Armstrong played with great enthusiasm and helped out with the arrangements. When the project was finished, he said, "I can't remember when I felt this good about making a record," according to Avakian's liner notes.

The album sold well enough to please Glaser, although it did little to alter what had by this time become the public's perception of Armstrong—that of the grinning showman they saw on television and in movies. Armstrong followed the Handy collection with 1955's *Satch Plays Fats*, featuring songs by jazz pianist and composer Fats Waller.

Avakian had wanted to put Armstrong in the studio with Duke Ellington, but the big-band collaboration album he envisioned was not to be. Glaser did not want his client to resign from Columbia—the contract that brought about the Handy album had, by this time, expired—and the manager told Avakian he would evaluate each subsequent offer on a project-by-project basis. Avakian balked, and Armstrong missed his chance to record with arguably the greatest jazz composer of all time.

Instead, Satchmo inked a deal with Verve Records, a label that specialized in "mainstream" jazz. Armstrong cut several winning Verve full-lengths, including three duets albums with acclaimed songstress Ella Fitzgerald. Under the supervision of Verve boss Norman Glanz, Armstrong cut neither the pop songs Decca required nor the jazz tunes that were Avakian's specialty. Backed by the Oscar Peterson Trio, he recorded sophisticated, slow-tempo show tunes and standards—songs that featured more singing than trumpet playing.

In 1956, hit films based on the lives of Benny Goodman and Glenn Miller signaled the public's renewed interest in figures from the big-band era. Looking ahead to a possible Armstrong biopic, Decca's Gabler endeavored to record new versions of the Hot Fives and Sevens and package them in a career-spanning retrospective—a collection that would serve as a companion piece to any Hollywood feature. Gabler hired arrangers to listen to Armstrong's original OKeh sides and transcribe the solos, although when it came time to record, he permitted the trumpeter to stray from his earlier parts as he saw fit.

Each night for the duration of the sessions, Gabler paid Armstrong and the All-Stars what they would have earned on the road, creating a situation whereby the musicians could fully commit to working on the collection. Eventually titled *Satchmo: A Musical Autobiography*, the set featured inter-song narrations from Armstrong, who told the stories behind each track. Serious jazz critics dismissed the set, pointing out the many ways in which the middle-aged Louis Armstrong failed to match the power of his younger self, but the jazzman nevertheless enjoyed his trip down Memory Lane.

Also in 1956, Armstrong and the All-Stars made their first trip to Africa, performing for 100,000 people in Ghana. The tour was sponsored by CBS, which sent a camera crew to shoot footage for what would become *Satchmo the Great,* a 1957 documentary produced by *See It Now* host and respected newsman Edward R. Murrow. The film ends with Armstrong performing alongside Leonard Bernstein and the New York Philharmonic Orchestra at New York City's Lewisohn Stadium.

## SPEAKING OUT

If the 1950s brought Armstrong unprecedented chart success and the adoration of fans around the world, the decade was not without its controversies. One of the most notorious episodes of Armstrong's career took place in September 1957, while the All-Stars were on tour in North Dakota. An industrious University of North Dakota journalism student named Larry Lubenow persuaded his editors at the *Grand Forks Herald* to let him write a story about the jazz great. Posing as a hotel worker, Lubenow snuck into Armstrong's room, then confessed to being a reporter and struck up a conversation with the characteristically friendly musician.

What began as innocent small talk soon turned to more serious matters. Earlier that week, angry white protestors had jeered at nine black students in Little Rock, Arkansas, preventing the youngsters from entering the city's Central High School. The students were merely exercising rights guaranteed under the U.S. Supreme Court's 1954 *Brown v. Board of Education* ruling, which struck down the "separate but equal" school segregation policy long in place throughout the South. Despite the high court's ruling, some whites were unwilling to accept the idea of mixed-race classrooms.

As the nation had watched tensions in Little Rock heat to a boil, Governor Orval Faubus of Arkansas had sided with the segregationists, sending the National Guard to block the black students from entering the school. President Dwight D. Eisenhower had met with the governor, but at the time of Armstrong's interview with Lubenow, the president had done

**In September 1957, troops from the 101st Airborne Division escort nine black students into Little Rock Central High School, in Little Rock, Arkansas, on the orders of President Dwight D. Eisenhower, who used the military to ensure that the school would be desegregated. In a rare foray into politics, Louis Armstrong was publicly critical of the president's initial response to the crisis.**

nothing to force Faubus's hand and make him comply with the Supreme Court's decision.

Armstrong was certainly no stranger to racism. In fact, at a recent show in Knoxville, Tennessee, white supremacists had thrown dynamite at the theater, momentarily disrupting his performance. Troubled by the Little Rock situation and angered by the federal government's inaction, Armstrong spoke frankly with Lubenow, treading into the political terrain he had spent years avoiding. He blasted Eisenhower, accusing the president of having "no guts," and referred to Faubus as an "uneducated plowboy." (His actual language was stronger, but this was as severe a putdown as Lubenow could print.)

Armstrong also told the young reporter he would cancel a "goodwill" tour of the Soviet Union he had agreed to undertake on behalf of the U.S. State Department. "It's getting almost so bad a colored man hasn't got any country," Armstrong said. "The people over there [in Russia] ask me what's wrong with my country, what am I supposed to say?"

Lubenow's editor demanded proof Armstrong had actually said such things, and the following day, the musician signed off on the quotes. The Associated Press then picked up Lubenow's story. As Armstrong made headlines across the country, several noteworthy African Americans, among them baseball great Jackie Robinson, came to his defense, offering similar admonitions of Eisenhower.

In an effort to save face, Armstrong's tour manager, Frenchy Tallerie, fed reporters a phony apology, an explanation said to have come from the musician himself. Having never much cared for Tallerie, Armstrong denied the apology and assured the press he had, indeed, meant everything he said.

Days later, Eisenhower "federalized" the Arkansas National Guard, taking them under his control, and deployed a separate batch of troops to ensure the "Little Rock Nine," as the students would become known, could enter the school. Some have speculated that the legendary musician played a role in spurring Eisenhower to action. Either way, a pleased Armstrong telegrammed the president, writing, "If you decide to walk into the schools with the little colored kids, take me along, Daddy. God bless you."

Although the incident did little to hurt Armstrong's career—he continued touring and making TV appearances as if nothing had happened—it did lead to a brief public war of words with entertainer Sammy Davis Jr., who called Armstrong a hypocrite and chided him for speaking out about the Little Rock situation even as he continued playing segregated concert halls. Glaser blasted back—"Who cares about Sammy Davis Jr.?" he asked, according to Collier—while Armstrong refused to comment.

A year earlier, Armstrong had responded to similar criticisms, telling a reporter he did not concern himself with where Glaser booked the band. He explained his reluctance to participate in civil rights marches by reiterating his credo: Above all else, he cared about music. However strongly he may have felt about the situation facing blacks in America, he was not going to let politics stand in the way of his career.

Even if Armstrong was not the outspoken civil rights crusader some critics wanted him to be, the truth was that he had done his part to protest the unfair treatment of his people. "As time went on and I made a reputation," he told Larry King in a 1967 interview for the magazine *Harper's*, "I had it put in my contracts that I wouldn't play no place I couldn't stay. I was the first Negro in the business to crack them big white hotels—Oh yeah! I pioneered, Pops!"

Moreover, from 1956 to 1965, a nine-year period in which Louisiana law prohibited black and white musicians from performing on the same stage, Armstrong refused to play New Orleans. His unwillingness to abide such racist laws was remarkable, especially when one considers the America he grew up in. As a poor black child in the South, Armstrong had experienced a level of racism well beyond that which existed in the 1950s and 1960s. That, for nearly a decade, he would steer clear of his hometown rather than submit to the status quo says a great deal about how much he had changed with the times.

Following the Little Rock hubbub, Armstrong kept his word and canceled his trip to the Soviet Union. Three years later, he finally did participate in a State Department goodwill tour, making his second trip to Africa, where he played for hundreds of thousands of fans. While in Sierra Leone, Velma Middleton died of a stroke, leaving Bigard as the lone remaining original All-Star. Six months later, he, too, left the band.

# 8

# Swinging Until the End

**Throughout the late 1950s,** Louis Armstrong continued touring vigorously. His lip was more fragile than ever, and he compensated by focusing on singing. On June 22, 1959, while in Italy recording a performance for *The Ed Sullivan Show,* he suffered a heart attack. When Armstrong returned home, he made an effort to eat better and to lose weight, and he also consented to cut back on his touring.

In 1961, Armstrong finally recorded with Duke Ellington, cutting the 10 sides that were to be their only collaborations. That same year, he traveled to France to film *Paris Blues,* which starred Paul Newman and Sidney Poitier. On May 23, 1963, he was among the artists to perform at a birthday tribute to President John F. Kennedy.

## "HELLO, DOLLY!"

All the while, Armstrong continued recording. In 1964, he again found success on the pop charts. A new musical version of the play *The Matchmaker* was headed for Broadway, and the show's producers enlisted Armstrong to record the song "Hello, Dolly!" in the hopes that it would drum up interest in the production.

Backed by a string section, Armstrong and the All-Stars cut a version Glaser knew immediately was going to be a hit. Bolstered by Armstrong's appearance on the TV show *What's My Line?* as well as by the success of its Broadway namesake, "Hello, Dolly!" climbed the charts from February to May, peaking at number one and dethroning the seemingly unbeatable Beatles, who had previously held the top spot with "Can't Buy Me Love."

Following the success of the "Hello, Dolly!" tune, which would earn Armstrong the distinction of being the oldest musician ever to top the *Billboard* Hot 100—a record that still stands—Satchmo returned to the studio to cut a cash-in album consisting largely of show tunes. Critics that had dismissed him years earlier praised the LP, *Louis Armstrong's "Hello, Dolly!"*, and *New York Times* writer John S. Wilson noted that the jazzman "still has his customary authority on trumpet."

In 1966, Armstrong made the cover of *Life*, and his 14-page interview was later released in book form. He found himself more beloved than ever. He appeared regularly on such TV programs as *The Tonight Show*, *The Dean Martin Show*, and *The Danny Kaye Show*. He continued to tour in a diminished capacity, feeding his ravenous appetite for the road. On those rare occasions that he followed his doctors' orders and took vacations, he was liable to cut his trips short, reassemble the All-Stars, and ask Glaser to book more shows.

His dogged work ethic was likely a product of his upbringing. On the streets of black Storyville, Armstrong learned early on that only the tenacious survive. Although he was now earn-

Louis Armstrong remained a popular entertainer throughout his life. Here, he is seen in a still taken from the 1969 musical *Hello, Dolly!*, in which he costarred with singer Barbra Streisand. His recording of the musical's title song became a popular hit.

ing hundreds of thousands of dollars a year, he remained the same man who, a half century earlier, had carted coal by day and played honky-tonks by night. He knew that show business offers no guarantees, and that audiences' tastes change. If he could just stay in the public eye, moving by bus from city to city, town to town, giving people a professional show, he reasoned, he could keep going forever. No one would have the chance to forget him.

## FINAL MASTERPIECES

In 1967, Armstrong recorded a song that, despite flopping at the time of its release, would be his last Top 40 hit. Penned by producer Bob Thiele in response to the uncertainties of the 1960s—a tumultuous decade marred by war, assassinations, and social upheavals—"What a Wonderful World" was intended as a song of hope. The sweet, sentimental ballad was perfect for Armstrong, who had always maintained a sunny disposition, even during the most difficult periods of his life.

Unfortunately, ABC Records head Larry Newton was unhappy with the recording and decided to cut promotion for the single, dooming it to failure. In 1988, thanks to its inclusion on the soundtrack to the hit film *Good Morning, Vietnam*, starring comedian Robin Williams, the song enjoyed a second life, climbing to number 32 on the *Billboard* Hot 100.

In 1968, Armstrong recorded what some critics consider his final great album, *Disney Songs the Satchmo Way*. If Armstrong had the slightest misgiving about cutting a children's record whose songs were originally made famous by cartoon characters, he did not let it affect his performance. Armstrong sings and plays trumpet with audible glee. Again demonstrating his ability to salvage questionable material, he turned the silly likes of "Heigh Ho" and "Bibbidi-Bobbidi-Boo" into joyful romps.

That same year, Armstrong made another trip to England and shot a duet with Barbra Streisand for the *Hello, Dolly!* film. That September, after he had lost a great deal of weight—60 pounds (27.2 kilograms), in his own estimation—he was diagnosed with congestive heart failure. His doctor wanted to hospitalize him immediately, but Armstrong waited two weeks before checking himself into New York City's Beth Israel Medical Center.

## LOSING A PARTNER

In the spring of 1969, while Armstrong was still in the hospital, Glaser suffered a stroke and went into a coma. Although he, too, was sent to Beth Israel, no one told Armstrong for fear the news would prove too devastating. The trumpeter eventually found out, however, after jazz musicians Tyree Glenn and Dizzy Gillespie let slip during a visit to Armstrong's room that they had just donated blood to Glaser.

Armstrong asked to be wheeled into Glaser's room and was saddened to find his manager unresponsive. Glaser died in June, by which time Armstrong had already returned to his home in Corona and begun his longest-ever period of downtime. He busied himself looking at photographs and newspaper clippings, listening to and making reel-to-reel recordings, and generally taking stock of a career that had spanned more than a half century.

Given all he had achieved, Armstrong might have finally settled down and rested on his laurels. He had a nice home and a faithful wife. For the first time in his life, he was putting down roots and becoming part of a community. He often spent time with neighborhood children, dined at a local Chinese restaurant, and got his hair cut at Joe's Artistic Barber Shop, never using his celebrity status to jump to the front of the line. Still, within his chest beat the heart of a restless entertainer, and the comfort of Corona was no substitute for the thrill of the road.

## EAGER TO PERFORM

In January 1970, after Glaser's management company renewed Armstrong's contract, the trumpeter wrote Oscar Cohen, the Glaser associate who had become his new boss, assuring him he was ready to resume touring. He told Cohen his sidemen had never been good enough, and that all they cared about was drinking and talking to chorus girls. Although it is possible Armstrong truly believed this, he may also have been trying to convince Cohen to line up another tour—a prospect that would have seemed more attractive if Armstrong could travel as a free agent, without the expense of a full band.

**Louis Armstrong performs in the United Kingdom late in his career. A consummate showman, Satchmo continued to record and perform until the last months of his life.**

Although Armstrong would play live again, he spent much of 1970 recording—he cut two albums, the poorly received group effort *Louis Armstrong and His Friends* and the genre exercise *Louis "Country & Western" Armstrong*—and celebrating his seventieth birthday. That year, he was the subject of countless newspaper and magazine articles, and the writer E.B. White penned a children's book, *The Trumpet of the Swan*, in his honor. In June, such musicians as Dizzy Gillespie, gospel star Mahalia Jackson, and the Eureka Brass Band paid tribute to Armstrong at the Newport Jazz Festival. Armstrong himself performed at the festival, and fans braved heavy rainfall to hear him play a medley of old favorites.

The final months of 1970 saw a flurry of activity, as Armstrong played shows in London, reassembled the All-Stars for a gig in Las Vegas, and once again made the talk-show rounds, chatting with Johnny Carson, Dick Cavett, and Flip Wilson, among others.

In March 1971, Armstrong signed on for two weeks of shows at New York City's Waldorf-Astoria hotel. To placate doctors who had advised against the engagement, Armstrong took a room at the Waldorf and came downstairs each night to play. He was noticeably weak, and at least one TV critic blasted his performance. Armstrong soldiered through the run of dates, and three days after what would prove the final performance of his career, he returned to Beth Israel, where he underwent a tracheotomy. By the summer, he had returned home to Corona, where he plotted yet another comeback.

## THE FINAL CURTAIN

This time, however, it was not to be. On July 6, 1971, two days after what he believed to be his seventy-first birthday, Armstrong died of a heart attack. As his body lay in state in Manhattan, some 25,000 fans paid their respects. Thousands more lined the streets outside of the Corona Congregational Church, where a who's who of celebrities were among those to attend his televised funeral. In addition to his good friend Bing Crosby, Armstrong's pallbearers included jazz greats Dizzy Gillespie, Duke Ellington, Ella Fitzgerald, and Count Basie, as well as TV personalities Ed Sullivan, Johnny Carson, and Merv Griffin.

Armstrong's was a somber, jazzless funeral—just the type he had asked for, a representative for his booking company told the press. Evidently, Armstrong had felt that if he let one jazz band play, he would have been obligated to "have all of them." A proper "jazz funeral"—the kind of raucous affair he had often taken part in as a young man in New Orleans—took place the following day in his hometown.

# 9

# Legacy of a Legend

**The death of Louis Armstrong was** an important-enough event that, upon hearing the news, President Richard Nixon issued a statement from aboard Air Force One. "Mrs. Nixon and I share the sorrow of millions of Americans at the death of Louis Armstrong," Nixon said. "One of the architects of an American art form, a free and individual spirit, and an artist of worldwide fame, his great talents and magnificent spirit added richness and pleasure to all our lives."

The day after his death, the *New York Times* ran a 4,000-word obituary. Writer Albin Krebs traced Armstrong's life from the slums of the Battlefield to the comforts of Corona, highlighting the trumpeter's many achievements. Although Krebs' piece was generally positive, it made mention of the divisive shift Armstrong's music had taken after 1928, when he cut the last of the Hot Fives. Krebs wrote:

His mugging, his wisecracking and most of all his willing-
ness to constantly repeat programs that had gone over well
in the past won him the cheers of his audiences, along with
the disapproving clucks of some of his fellow musicians and
jazz specialists.

## A CONTENTIOUS LEGACY

From 1971 onward, Armstrong's legacy has been a source of
debate among jazz critics and aficionados. Although some
maintain that he ceased being a relevant artist around the time
he turned his attention to pop music, others treasure his post-
1920s output and insist that Satchmo continued recording
high-quality music until the end of his life.

In his 1983 book *Louis Armstrong: An American Genius*, the
first major biography published after the trumpeter's death,
Collier mixed praise with criticism, lamenting "the bitter waste
of his astonishing talent over the last two-thirds of his career."
"I cannot think of another American artist who so failed his
own talent," Collier writes. "What went wrong?" According
to Collier, Armstrong suffered two major flaws. The first was
cultural: Armstrong saw himself as an entertainer, not a serious artist. This trap, Collier wrote, was a product of the black

## IN HIS OWN WORDS...

Although Louis Armstrong was capable of stunning musical innovations, he
never aspired to play simply for jazz critics and musicologists. After cutting the
wildly inventive Hot Fives, Satchmo spent the bulk of his career focusing on
more audience-friendly material, both onstage and on record. He did this not to
make money, but rather to make fans happy, as is evident from this quote from
his *New York Times* obituary: "I never tried to prove nothing, just wanted to
give a good show. My life has always been my music, it's always come first, but
the music ain't worth nothing if you can't lay it on the public. The main thing is
to live for that audience, 'cause what you're there for is to please the people."

experience. Due to pervasive racism, the author theorized, many talented blacks of Armstrong's time felt compelled to smile big, roll their eyes, and demean themselves for the pleasure of white audiences. It was the only way they thought they would be accepted.

Armstrong's second flaw, according to Collier, was his "desperate need to hang onto the boundless love his audiences offered him." Whereas some viewed this as Armstrong's greatest charm—should he really be criticized for wanting to make people happy?—Collier accuses Satchmo of resorting to "obvious trickery," such as blowing those dizzying runs of high-C notes, and making music "not nearly up to what he could have created."

## THE RESPECT OF HIS PEERS

Others in the jazz community, such as trumpeter Wynton Marsalis, have taken a more favorable view of Armstrong's career. In 1991, when Marsalis became director of New York City's Jazz at Lincoln Center program, he began featuring Armstrong's music, helping introduce Satchmo to a new generation of listeners. Marsalis was among those who praised Armstrong in filmmaker Ken Burns's 10-part *Jazz*, a 2001 PBS documentary series that portrayed Armstrong as one of the genre's seminal figures.

Of course, Armstrong had always been respected among fellow jazz musicians, even those with radically different approaches to music. "You can't play nothing on trumpet that doesn't come from him," Miles Davis, who had previously taken issue with Armstrong's showmanlike ways, once said, adding, "I can't ever remember a time when he sounded bad playing the trumpet. Never." Asked about Armstrong's penchant for mugging and singing popular or silly songs, Billie Holiday offered this defense: "Of course Pops toms, but he toms from the heart." "If anybody was Mr. Jazz it was Louis Armstrong," Duke Ellington was quoted as saying in Krebs's

The U.S. Postal Service honored Louis Armstrong with the release of this commemorative stamp in September 1995. It was part of a set of 10 stamps honoring jazz greats.

*Times* obituary. "He was the epitome of jazz and always will be. He is what I call an American standard, an American original."

### FOREVER A SUPERSTAR

Most of the battles over Armstrong's supposed tomming and post-Hot Fives recordings have been fought by critics, musicologists, and serious students of jazz music. In the eyes of casual listeners, especially those who grew up during the time when "Hello, Dolly!" was ubiquitous on the radio, Armstrong remains a beloved entertainer. In 1995, the U.S. Postal Service issued a commemorative stamp, and six years later, on the one-hundredth anniversary of Satchmo's birth, the city of

New Orleans renamed its airport Louis Armstrong International, adding to the list of local monuments already bearing his name.

One need only attend a wedding reception or high school prom to confirm the enduring popularity of "What a Wonderful World," perhaps Armstrong's best-known performance, at least among young people. In 2002, punk-rock singer Joey Ramone recorded a version for his album *Don't Worry About Me.* Nearly a decade earlier, the Los Angeles hip-hop group Cypress Hill name-checked Armstrong in its 1994 hit "Insane in the Brain," tying Satchmo back to a genre that, with the 1940 recording "You've Got Me Voodoo'd," biographer Gary Giddins argues, he may have helped create.

## A PERMANENT MONUMENT

Lucille Armstrong never remarried and lived in Corona for the remainder of her life. She died in 1983, leaving the home she and Armstrong once shared to the New York City Department of Cultural Affairs. Stewardship of the house then passed to Queens College. In 1991, the school began archiving Armstrong's

### DID YOU KNOW?

In 1915, as if he did not already have his hands full providing for his mother and sister, a teenage Louis Armstrong found himself supporting a third family member, Clarence, the son of his cousin Flora, who had died soon after giving birth to the boy. One rainy day, Clarence slipped on the wooden floor of the family's second-story balcony and fell to the ground, sustaining severe head injuries. Armstrong adopted the mentally impaired boy and cared for him throughout his life. Satchmo never had children of his own, and by all accounts, he delighted in referring to Clarence as "Little Louis Armstrong." In order to keep Clarence from being institutionalized, the jazzman arranged for him to "marry" an older woman named Evelyn Hadfield, who served as his caretaker. Clarence survived Louis by more than two decades, dying in the Bronx, New York, in 1998.

Louis Armstrong's house in the Corona neighborhood of Queens, New York. After her death, Lucille Armstrong left the home and its contents to the New York City Department of Cultural Affairs, including more than 650 personal tapes recorded by the late king of jazz, each more than four hours long. Today, the Louis Armstrong House Museum is open to the public.

massive collection of tapes, writings, and other belongings.

The Louis Armstrong Archives opened to the public in 1994. In 2003, the newly renovated house—recast as the Louis Armstrong House Museum—opened for public tours, giving fans a chance to see the house as it looked in the trumpeter's time. Construction on a new visitors center began in 2007, and the museum often stages concerts and lectures.

The museum's Web site features a calendar of events, a timeline of Armstrong's life and achievements, and a listing of his many films and recordings. Posted on the site is a quote from legendary singer Tony Bennett, one that, in the eyes of Satchmo's fans around the world, sums up the story of the great jazzman: "The bottom line of any country is: what did we contribute to the world? . . . We contributed Louis Armstrong."

# Selected Discography

The following are a selection of some of the more highly regarded Louis Armstrong albums and compilations:

**1956** *Louis Armstrong Plays W.C. Handy*

**1997** *The Complete Ella Fitzgerald & Louis Armstrong on Verve*

**2000** *Hello, Dolly!*

**2004** *The Essential Louis Armstrong*

**2008** *The Best of the Hot Fives & Sevens*

**1901** Born August 4 in New Orleans, Louisiana; baptized three weeks later at the Sacred Heart of Jesus Church, a white Roman Catholic Church; goes to live with his paternal grandmother, Josephine.

**1905 or 1906** Goes to live with his mother and sister in "black Storyville" section of New Orleans.

**1907** Begins singing on street corners as part of a vocal quartet, earning praise from local musicians; uses money borrowed from the Karnofskys, the Jewish family he works for, to purchase his first cornet.

**1912** Arrested for firing a pistol on New Year's Eve and spends the night in jail.

**1913** Sent to the Colored Waif's Home for Boys, where, under the tutelage of Peter Davis, he hones his cornet skills and develops a love and appreciation for various forms of music; performs in street parades.

**1918** Quits his day job pushing coal carts and becomes a full-time musician; marries his first wife, Daisy, a strong-willed prostitute known to carry a razor; begins performing on Mississippi River excursion boats, learning from bandleader Fate Marable how to read music and improvise solos.

**1922** Receives an invitation from his mentor, Joe "King" Oliver, to move to Chicago and join the Creole Jazz Band; leaves New Orleans on August 8; makes his debut with Oliver's group the following day.

**1923** Makes first recordings with Creole Jazz Band.

**1924** Marries his second wife, Lil Hardin, and, on her urging, quits King Oliver's band; moves to New York City and joins the Fletcher Henderson Orchestra; records with a series of female blues singers.

**1925** Moves back to Chicago and begins performing at the Dreamland Café, where he is billed as "The World's Greatest Cornet Player;" leads his own band, the Hot Five, on the first in a series of seminal OKeh label recordings that will revolutionize jazz.

**1927** With the addition of drums and tuba, rechristens the Hot Five "the Hot Seven" and cuts a number of classic sides, including "Potato Head Blues," one of his most revered recordings; his mother dies in New Orleans.

**1928** Records the last of the Hot Fives, including "West End Blues," a song many consider to be his masterpiece.

**1932** Makes first trip to England, where he acquires the nickname "Satchmo"; performs at the London Palladium; completes a three-month tour of Great Britain; splits lip at New Year's Eve performance in Baltimore, Maryland.

**1935** Hires Joe Glaser, the tough-talking businessman who will serve as his manager for more than three decades.

**1936** Makes Hollywood debut, appearing with friend Bing Crosby in *Pennies from Heaven*; releases autobiography, *Swing That Music*.

**1938** Divorces Lil and marries third wife, Alpha Smith.

**1942** Divorces Alpha and marries Lucille Wilson, his fourth and final wife.

**1947** Leads jazz sextets at New York City's Carnegie Hall and Town Hall, marking the end of his big-band days and triumphant return to small-group jazz; forms the All-Stars, the group he will front for the remainder of his career.

**1956** Scores chart hits with "Blueberry Hill" and "Mack the Knife."

**1957** Speaks out against mistreatment of black high school students in Little Rock, Arkansas, in interview with North Dakota newspaper; cancels planned U.S. State Department goodwill trip to Russia; faces criticism from Sammy Davis Jr., who accuses Armstrong of being hypocritical on race issues; releases *Satchmo: A Musical Autobiography*, a four-LP set in which he tells the story of his life and leads the All-Stars through updated versions of his classic recordings.

**1959**   Suffers a heart attack in Italy.

**1964**   Tops the *Billboard* Hot 100 with "Hello, Dolly!" and knocks the Beatles' "Can't Buy Me Love" out of the top slot.

**1970**   Celebrates what is thought to be his seventieth birthday with star-studded Newport Jazz Festival tribute; plays concerts in London and Las Vegas and appears on numerous talk shows.

**1971**   Performs two weeks of shows at New York City's Waldorf-Astoria hotel, despite objections from doctors; dies of a heart attack on July 6.

**1991**   Queens College begins cataloguing Armstrong's enormous collection of recordings, writings, and personal belongings; the school opens the Louis Armstrong Archives to the public three years later.

**1995**   U.S. Postal Service issues Armstrong commemorative stamp.

**2003**   The Louis Armstrong House Museum in Queens, New York, opens for public tours.

# Further Reading

Armstrong, Louis. *Satchmo: My Life in New Orleans.* New York: Prentice-Hall, 1954.

———. *Swing That Music.* London and New York: Longmans, Green, 1936.

Armstrong, Louis, and Thomas Brothers, ed. *Louis Armstrong, In His Own Words: Selected Writings.* New York: Oxford University Press, 1999.

Brothers, Thomas. *Louis Armstrong's New Orleans.* New York: W. W. Norton & Company, Inc., 2006.

Brower, Steven. *Satchmo: The Wonderful World and Art of Louis Armstrong.* New York: Abrams, 2009.

Collier, James Lincoln. *Louis Armstrong: An American Genius.* New York: Oxford University Press, 1983.

Giddins, Gary. *Satchmo: The Genius of Louis Armstrong.* New York: Da Capo Press, 2001.

Meckna, Michael. *Satchmo: The Louis Armstrong Encyclopedia.* Westport, Conn.: Greenwood Press, 2004.

Teachout, Terry. *Pops: A Life of Louis Armstrong.* New York: Houghton Mifflin Harcourt, 2009.

## WEB SITES

**Jazz by Ken Burns: Louis Armstrong biography**
http://www.pbs.org/jazz/biography/artist_id_armstrong_louis.htm

**Louis Armstrong Discography**
http://www.michaelminn.net/armstrong/

**Louis Armstrong House Museum**
http://www.louisarmstronghouse.org/

**Louis "Satchmo" Armstrong biography**
http://www.redhotjazz.com/louie.html

**Rock and Roll Hall of Fame: Louis Armstrong Biography**
http://www.rockhall.com/inductee/louis-armstrong

page

# About the Author

**Kenneth Partridge** is a freelance journalist based in Brooklyn, New York. He has written extensively about music and pop culture for such publications as the *Village Voice, USA Today,* Spinner.com, UGO.com, *Electronic Musician, Performing Songwriter,* and the *Hartford Courant,* Connecticut's largest daily newspaper. Partridge also works as an editor at the H.W. Wilson Company, a library reference publisher. Prior to moving to New York, he covered local news for the *Greenwich Post,* a weekly newspaper in Greenwich, Connecticut, and wrote grants for a youth-serving nonprofit organization. He holds a degree in economics from Boston University.